ANGELS IN AMERICA

A Gay Fantasia on National Themes

PART ONE: MILLENNIUM APPROACHES

Tony Kushner

BROADWAY PLAY PUBLISHING INC
224 E 62nd St, NY, NY 10065
www.broadwayplaypub.com
info@broadwayplaypub.com

I S B N: 978-0-88145-651-6

First printing: January 2017

Typographic controls: Adobe InDesign
Typeface: Adobe Caslon
Printed and bound in the U S A

ANGELS IN AMERICA, PART ONE: MILLENNIUM APPROACHES was first performed in a workshop production presented by Center Theatre Group/Mark Taper Forum, May 1990.

The world premiere was presented by The Eureka Theatre Company, May 1991.

Opened in London at the Royal National Theatre of Great Britain, January 1992.

Opened in New York at the Walter Kerr Theatre in April 1993.

The first production of ANGELS IN AMERICA, PARTS ONE AND TWO was presented at the Mark Taper Forum, November 1992.

THE CHARACTERS
IN *MILLENNIUM APPROACHES*

ROY M. COHN,* a successful New York lawyer and unofficial power broker.

JOSEPH PORTER PITT, chief clerk for Justice Theodore Wilson of the Federal Court of Appeals, Second Circuit.

HARPER AMATY PITT, Joe's wife, an agoraphobic with a mild Valium addiction.

LOUIS IRONSON, a word processor working for the Second Circuit Court of Appeals.

PRIOR WALTER, Louis's boyfriend. Occasionally works as a club designer or caterer, otherwise lives very modestly but with great style off a small trust fund.

HANNAH PORTER PITT, Joe's mother, currently residing in Salt Lake City, living off her deceased husband's army pension.

BELIZE, a registered nurse and former drag queen whose name was originally Norman Arriaga; Belize is a drag name that stuck.

THE ANGEL, four divine emanations, Fluor, Phosphor, Lumen and Candle; manifest in One: the Continental Principality of America. She has magnificent steel-gray wings.

Other Characters in Millennium Approaches

RABBI ISIDOR CHEMELWITZ, an orthodox Jewish rabbi, played by the actor playing Hannah.

MR. LIES, Harper's imaginary friend, a travel agent, played by the actor playing Belize. In style of dress and speech he suggests a jazz musician; he always wears a large lapel badge emblazoned "IOTA" (International Order of Travel Agents).

THE MAN IN THE PARK, played by the actor playing Prior.

THE VOICE, the voice of the Angel.

HENRY, Roy's doctor, played by the actor playing Hannah.

EMILY, a nurse, played by the actor playing the Angel.

MARTIN HELLER, a Reagan Administration Justice Department flackman, played by the actor playing Harper.

SISTER ELLA CHAPTER, a Salt Lake City real-estate saleswoman, played by the actor playing the Angel.

PRIOR 1, the ghost of a dead Prior Walter from the thirteenth century, played by the actor playing Joe. A blunt, grim, dutiful, medieval farmer, he speaks abruptly and rather loudly with a guttural Yorkshire accent.

PRIOR 2, the ghost of a dead Prior Walter from the seventeenth century, played by the actor playing Roy. A Londoner, a Restoration-era sophisticate and bon vivant; he speaks with an elegant Received English accent.

THE ESKIMO, played by the actor playing Joe.

A HOMELESS WOMAN, an unmedicated psychotic who lives on the streets of the South Bronx; played by the actor playing the Angel.

ETHEL ROSENBERG, played by the actor playing Hannah.

* The character Roy M. Cohn is based on the late Roy M. Cohn (1927–1986), who was all too real; for the most part the acts attributed to the character Roy, such as his illegal conferences with Judge Kaufmann during the trial of Ethel Rosenberg, are to be found in the historical record. But this Roy is a work of dramatic fiction; his words are my invention, and liberties have been taken.

Millennium Approaches *is dedicated to*
Mark Bronnenberg

In a murderous time
  the heart breaks and breaks
    and lives by breaking.

—STANLEY KUNITZ, "The Testing-Tree"

ACT ONE:

Bad News

October–November 1985

Scene 1

The end of October. Rabbi Isidor Chemelwitz alone onstage with a small coffin. It is a rough pine box with two wooden pegs, one at the foot and one at the head, holding the lid in place. A prayer shawl embroidered with a Star of David is draped over the lid, and at the head of the coffin, a yahrzeit candle is burning.

The Rabbi speaks sonorously, with a heavy Eastern European accent, unapologetically consulting a sheet of notes for the family names.

RABBI ISIDOR CHEMELWITZ: Hello and good morning. I am Rabbi Isidor Chemelwitz of the Bronx Home for Aged Hebrews. We are here this morning to pay respects at the passing of Sarah Ironson, devoted wife of Benjamin Ironson, also deceased, loving and caring mother of her sons Morris, Abraham, and Samuel, and her daughters

Esther and Rachel; beloved grandmother of Max, Mark, Louis, Lisa, Maria . . . uh . . . Lesley, Angela, Doris, Luke and Eric. *(Looks closer at paper)* Eric? This is a Jewish name? *(Shrugs)* Eric. A large and loving family. We assemble that we may mourn collectively this good and righteous woman.

(He looks at the coffin)

This woman. I did not know this woman. I cannot accurately describe her attributes, nor do justice to her dimensions. She was . . . Well, in the Bronx Home for Aged Hebrews are many like this, the old, and to many I speak but not to be frank with this one. She preferred silence. So I do not know her and yet I know her. She was . . . *(He touches the coffin)* . . . not a person but a whole kind of person, the ones who crossed the ocean, who brought with us to America the villages of Russia and Lithuania—and how we struggled, and how we fought, for the family, for the Jewish home, so that you would not grow up *here*, in this strange place, in the melting pot where nothing melted. Descendants of this immigrant woman, you do not grow up in America, you and your children and their children with the goyische names, you do not live in America, no such place exists. Your clay is the clay of some Litvak shtetl, your air the air of the steppes. Because she carried the old world on her back across the ocean, in a boat, and she put it down on Grand Concourse Avenue, or in Flatbush, and she worked that earth into your bones, and you pass it to your children, this ancient, ancient culture and home.

(Little pause)

You can never make that crossing that she made, for such Great Voyages in this world do not any more exist. But every day of your lives the miles that voyage between that place and this one you cross. Every day. You understand me? In you that journey is.

So . . .

She was the last of the Mohicans, this one was. Pretty soon . . . all the old will be dead.

Scene 2

Same day. Roy and Joe in Roy's office. Roy at an impressive desk, bare except for a very elaborate phone system, rows and rows of flashing buttons that bleep and beep and whistle incessantly, making chaotic music underneath Roy's conversations. Joe is sitting, waiting. Roy conducts business with great energy, impatience and sensual abandon: gesticulating, shouting, cajoling, crooning, playing the phone's receiver, its hold button and the buttons for its numerous lines with virtuosity and love.

ROY *(Hitting the hold button)*: Hold. *(To Joe)* I wish I was an octopus, a fucking octopus. Eight loving arms and all those suckers. Know what I mean?

JOE: No, I—

ROY *(Gesturing to a deli platter of little sandwiches on his desk)*: You want lunch?

JOE: No, that's OK really I just—

ROY *(Hitting a button)*: Ailene? Roy Cohn. Now what kind of a greeting is—I thought we were friends, Ai— Look Mrs. Soffer you don't have to get— You're upset. You're yelling. You'll aggravate your condition, you shouldn't yell, you'll pop little blood vessels in your face if you yell— No that was a joke, Mrs. Soffer, I was joking—I already apologized sixteen times for that, Mrs. Soffer,

3

you . . . *(While she's fulminating, Roy covers the mouthpiece with his hand and talks to Joe)* This'll take a minute, *eat* already, what is this tasty sandwich here it's— *(He takes a bite of a sandwich)* Mmmmm, liver or some— Here. *(He pitches the sandwich to Joe, who catches it and returns it to the platter. Back to Mrs. Soffer)* Uh-huh, uh-huh . . . No, I already told you it wasn't a vacation it was business, Mrs. Soffer, I have clients in Haiti, Mrs. Soffer, I— Listen, Ailene, YOU THINK I'M THE ONLY GODDAMN LAWYER IN HISTORY EVER MISSED A COURT DATE?! Don't make such a big fucking— Hold. *(He hits the hold button)* You HAG!

JOE: If this is a bad time—

ROY: *Bad* time? This is a *good* time! *(Button)* Baby doll, get me— Oh fuck, wait. *(Button)* Hello? Yah. Sorry to keep you holding, Judge Hollins, I— Oh *Mrs.* Hollins, sorry dear, deep voice you got. Enjoying your visit? *(Hand over mouthpiece again; to Joe)* She sounds like a truck driver and he sounds like Kate Smith, very confusing. Nixon appointed him, all the geeks are Nixon appointees. *(To Mrs. Hollins)* Yeah, yeah right good so how many tickets dear? *Seven?* For what, *Cats, 42nd Street*, what? No you wouldn't like *La Cage*, trust me, I know. Oh for godsake. Hold. *(Hold button, button)* Baby doll, seven for *Cats* or something, anything hard to get, I don't give a fuck what and neither will they. *(Button; to Joe)* You see *La Cage*?

JOE: No, I—

ROY: Fabulous. Best thing on Broadway. Maybe ever. *(Button)* Who? Aw, Jesus H. Christ, Harry, *no*, Harry, Judge John Francis Grimes, Manhattan Family Court. Do I have to do every goddamn thing myself? *Touch* the bastard, Harry, and don't call me on this line again, I told you not to.

JOE *(Starting to get up)*: Roy, uh, should I wait outside or—

ROY *(To Joe)*: Oh sit. *(To Harry)* You hold. I pay you to hold fuck you Harry you jerk. Half-wit dick-brain. *(Hold button, then he looks at Joe. A beat, then:)*

I see the universe, Joe, as a kind of sandstorm in outer space with winds of mega-hurricane velocity, but instead of grains of sand it's shards and splinters of glass. You ever feel that way? Ever have one of those days?

JOE: I'm not sure I—

ROY: So how's life in Appeals? How's the judge?

JOE: He sends his best.

ROY: He's a good man. Loyal. Not the brightest man on the bench, but he has manners. And a nice head of silver hair.

JOE: He gives me a lot of responsibility.

ROY: Yeah, like writing his decisions and signing his name.

JOE: Well . . .

ROY: He's a nice guy. And you cover admirably.

JOE: Well, thanks, Roy, I—   *pauses*

ROY *(Button)*: Yah? Who is *this*? Well who the fuck are *you*? Hold. *(Hold button)* Harry? Eighty-seven grand, something like that. Fuck him. Eat me. New Jersey, chain of porno film stores in, uh, Weehawken. That's—Harry, that's the beauty of the law. *(Hold button, button)* So, baby doll, what? *Cats?* Ugh. *(Button) Cats!* It's about cats. Singing cats, you'll love it. Eight o'clock, the theater's always at eight. *(Button)* Fucking tourists. *(He puts his finger on the button for the line on which Harry is holding; before pushing it, to Joe)* Oh live a little, Joe, *eat* something for Christ sake.

JOE: Um, Roy, could you—

ROY: What? *(Pushing the button; to Harry)* Hold a minute. *(Hold button, button)* Mrs. Soffer? Mrs.— *(Button, to Baby Doll)* God-fucking-damnit to hell, where is— *(Continue below:)*

JOE: Roy, I'd really appreciate it if—

ROY *(Continuous from above)*: Well she was here a minute ago, baby doll, see if—

(The phone starts making three different beeping sounds, all at once.)

ROY *(Smashing buttons)*: Jesus fuck this goddamn thing! *(Continue below:)*

JOE: I really wish you wouldn't—

ROY *(Continuous from above)*: Baby doll? Ring the *Post* get me Suzy see if—

(The phone starts whistling loudly.)

ROY: CHRIST!

JOE: *Roy.*

ROY *(Into receiver)*: Hold. *(Hold button; to Joe) What?*

JOE: Could you please not take the Lord's name in vain?

(Pause.)

JOE: I'm sorry. But please. At least while I'm . . .

ROY *(Laughs, then)*: Right. Sorry. Fuck.

Only in America. *(Punches a button)* Baby doll, tell 'em all to fuck off. Tell 'em I died. You handle Mrs. Soffer. Tell her it's on the way. Tell her I'm schtupping the judge. I'll call her back. I *will* call her. I *know* how much I borrowed. She's got four hundred times that stuffed up her— Yeah, tell her I said that.

(Button. The phone is silent)

So Joe.

JOE: I'm sorry Roy, I just—

ROY: No no no no, principles count, I respect principles, I'm not religious but I like God and God likes me. Baptist, Catholic?

JOE: Mormon.

ROY: Mormon. Delectable. Absolutely. Only in America. So, Joe. Whattya think?

JOE: It's . . . well . . .

ROY: Crazy life.

JOE: Chaotic.

ROY: Well but God bless chaos. Right?

JOE: Ummm . . .

ROY: Huh. Mormons. I knew Mormons, in, um, Nevada.

JOE: Utah, mostly.

ROY: No, these Mormons were in Vegas.

So. So, how'd you like to go to Washington and work for the Justice Department?

JOE: Sorry?

ROY: How'd you like to go to Washington and work for the Justice Department? All I gotta do is pick up the phone, talk to Ed, and you're in.

JOE: In . . . what, exactly?

ROY: Associate Assistant Something Big. Internal Affairs, heart of the woods, something nice with clout.

JOE: Ed . . . ?

ROY: Meese. The Attorney General.

JOE: Oh.

ROY: I just have to pick up the phone . . .

JOE: I have to think.

ROY: Of course.

(Pause)

It's a great time to be in Washington, Joe.

JOE: Roy, it's incredibly exciting.

ROY: And it would mean something to me. You understand?

(Little pause.)

JOE: I . . . can't say how much I appreciate this Roy, I'm sort of . . . well, stunned, I mean . . . Thanks, Roy. But I have to give it some thought. I have to ask my wife.
ROY: Your wife. Of course.
JOE: But I really appreciate—
ROY: Of course. Talk to your wife.

Scene 3

Same day. Harper at home, alone, as she often is, listening to the radio. She speaks to the audience:

HARPER: People who are lonely, people left alone, sit talking nonsense to the air, imagining . . . beautiful systems dying, old fixed orders spiraling apart.

When you look at the ozone layer, from outside, from a spaceship, it looks like a pale blue halo, a gentle, shimmering aureole encircling the atmosphere encircling the earth. Thirty miles above our heads, a thin layer of three-atom oxygen molecules, product of photosynthesis, which explains the fussy vegetable preference for visible light, its rejection of darker rays and emanations. Danger from without. It's a kind of gift, from God, the crowning touch to the creation of the world: guardian angels, hands linked, make a spherical net, a blue-green nesting orb, a shell of safety for life itself. But everywhere, things are collapsing, lies surfacing, systems of defense giving way.

This is why, Joe, this is why I shouldn't be left alone.
(Little pause)

I'd like to go traveling. Leave you behind to worry. I'll send postcards with strange stamps and tantalizing messages on the back: "Later maybe." "Nevermore . . ."

(Mr. Lies, a travel agent, appears, carrying a briefcase.)

HARPER: Oh! You startled me!

MR. LIES: Cash, check or credit card?

HARPER: I remember you. You're from Salt Lake. You sold us the plane tickets when we flew here. What are you doing in Brooklyn?

MR. LIES: You said you wanted to travel . . .

HARPER: And here you are. How thoughtful.

MR. LIES: Mr. Lies. Of the International Order of Travel Agents. We mobilize the globe, we set people adrift, we stir the populace and send nomads eddying across the planet. We are adepts of motion, acolytes of the flux. Cash, check or credit card. Name your destination.

HARPER: Antarctica, maybe. I want to see the hole in the ozone. I heard on the radio—

(He opens his briefcase. Inside it, there is a computer terminal.)

MR. LIES *(His hands poised over the keyboard)*: I can arrange a guided tour. Now?

HARPER: Soon. Maybe soon. I'm not safe here you see. Things aren't right with me. Weird stuff happens.

MR. LIES: Like?

HARPER: Well, like you, for instance. Just appearing. Or last week . . . well never mind.

People are like planets, you need a thick skin. Things get to me, Joe stays away and now . . . Well look. My dreams are talking back to me.

MR. LIES: It's the price of rootlessness. Motion sickness. The only cure: to keep moving.

HARPER: I'm undecided. I feel . . . that something's going to give. It's 1985. Fifteen years till the third millennium. Maybe Christ will come again. Maybe seeds will be planted, maybe there'll be harvests then, maybe early figs to eat, maybe new life, maybe fresh blood, maybe companionship and love and protection, safety from what's outside, maybe the door will hold, or maybe . . . Maybe the troubles will come, and the end will come, and the sky will collapse and there will be terrible rains and showers of poison light, or maybe my life is really fine, maybe Joe loves me and I'm only crazy thinking otherwise, or maybe not, maybe it's even worse than I know, maybe . . . I want to know, maybe I don't. The suspense, Mr. Lies, it's killing me.

MR. LIES: I suggest a vacation.

HARPER (Hearing something): That was the elevator. Oh God, I should fix myself up, I— You have to go, you shouldn't be here, you aren't even real.

MR. LIES: Call me when you decide.

HARPER: Go!

(Mr. Lies vanishes as Joe enters.)

JOE: Buddy?
    Buddy? Sorry I'm late. I was just . . . out. Walking. Are you mad?

HARPER: I got a little anxious.

JOE: Buddy kiss.

(They kiss.)

JOE: Nothing to get anxious about.
    So. So how'd you like to move to Washington?

Scene 4

Same day. Louis and Prior sitting outside on a bench near an Upper West Side funeral home, both dressed in funereal finery; Prior is elegant, Louis is rumpled/negligent. The funeral service for Sarah Ironson has just concluded and Louis is about to leave for the cemetery.

LOUIS: My grandmother actually saw Emma Goldman speak. In Yiddish. But all Grandma could remember was that she spoke well and wore a hat.

What a weird service. That rabbi.

PRIOR: A definite find. Get his number when you go to the graveyard. I want him to bury me.

LOUIS: Better head out there. Everyone gets to put dirt on the coffin once it's lowered in.

PRIOR: Oooh. Cemetery fun. Don't want to miss that.

LOUIS: It's an old Jewish custom to express love. Here, Grandma, have a shovelful. Latecomers run the risk of finding the grave completely filled.

She was pretty crazy. She was up there in that home for ten years, talking to herself. I never visited. She looked too much like my mother.

PRIOR *(Hugs him)*: Poor Louis. I'm sorry your grandma is dead.

LOUIS: Tiny little coffin, huh?

Sorry I didn't introduce you to— I always get so closety at these family things.

PRIOR: Butch. You get butch. *(Imitating)* "Hi, Cousin Doris, you don't remember me I'm Lou, Rachel's boy." Lou, not Louis, because if you say Louis they'll hear the sibilant S.

LOUIS: I don't have a—

PRIOR: I don't blame you, hiding. Bloodlines. Jewish curses are the worst. I personally would dissolve if anyone ever looked me in the eye and said "Feh." Fortunately WASPs don't say "Feh." Oh and by the way, darling, Cousin Doris is a dyke.

LOUIS: No.
    Really?

PRIOR: You don't notice anything. If I hadn't spent the last four years fellating you I'd swear you were straight.

LOUIS: You're in a pissy mood. Cat still missing?

(Little pause.)

PRIOR: Not a furball in sight. It's your fault.

LOUIS: It is?

PRIOR: I warned you, Louis. Names are important. Call an animal Little Sheba and you can't expect it to stick around. Besides, it's a dog's name.

LOUIS: I wanted a dog in the first place, not a cat. He sprayed my books.

PRIOR: He was a female cat.

LOUIS: Cats are stupid, high-strung predators. Babylonians sealed them up in bricks. Dogs have brains.

PRIOR: Cats have intuition.

LOUIS: A sharp dog is as smart as a really dull two-year-old child.

PRIOR: Cats know when something's wrong.

LOUIS: Only if you stop feeding them.

PRIOR: They know. That's why Sheba left, because she knew.

LOUIS: Knew what?

(Pause.)

PRIOR: I did my best Shirley Booth this morning, floppy slippers, housecoat, curlers, can of Little Friskies: "Come back, Little Sheba, come back . . ." To no avail. Le chat, elle ne reviendra jamais, jamais . . .

(He removes his jacket, rolls up his sleeve, shows Louis a dark purple spot on the underside of his arm near the shoulder.)

PRIOR: See.

LOUIS: That's just a burst blood vessel.

PRIOR: Not according to the best medical authorities.

LOUIS: What?

> *(Pause)*
> Tell me.

PRIOR: K.S., baby. Lesion number one. Lookit. The wine-dark kiss of the angel of death.

LOUIS *(Very softly, holding Prior's arm)*: Oh please . . .

PRIOR: I'm a lesionnaire. The Foreign Lesion. The American Lesion. Lesionnaire's disease.

LOUIS: Stop.

PRIOR: My troubles are lesion.

LOUIS: Will you *stop*.

PRIOR: Don't you think I'm handling this well?

> I'm going to die.

LOUIS: Bullshit.

PRIOR: Let go of my arm.

LOUIS: No.

PRIOR: Let go.

LOUIS *(Grabbing Prior, embracing him ferociously)*: No.

PRIOR: I can't find a way to spare you, baby. No wall like the wall of hard scientific fact. K.S. Wham. Bang your head on that.

LOUIS: Fuck you. *(Letting go)* Fuck you fuck you fuck you.

PRIOR: Now that's what I like to hear. A mature reaction.
Let's go see if the cat's come home.
Louis?
LOUIS: When did you find this?
PRIOR: I couldn't tell you.
LOUIS: Why?
PRIOR: I was scared, Lou.
LOUIS: Of what?
PRIOR: That you'll leave me.
LOUIS: Oh.

(Little pause.)

PRIOR: Bad timing, funeral and all, but I figured as long as
we're on the subject of death.
LOUIS: I have to go bury my grandma.
PRIOR: Lou?
(Pause)
Then you'll come home?
LOUIS: Then I'll come home.

Scene 5

Same day. Split scene: Joe and Harper at home, as before; Louis at the cemetery after his family has gone, lingering behind, staring down at Sarah Ironson's coffin in her open grave.

HARPER: Washington?
JOE: It's an incredible honor, buddy, and—
HARPER: I have to think.

JOE: Of course.

HARPER: Say no.

JOE: You said you were going to think about it.

HARPER: I don't want to move to Washington.

JOE: Well I do.

HARPER: It's a giant cemetery, huge white graves and mauso-
leums everywhere.

JOE: We could live in Maryland. Or Georgetown.

HARPER: We're happy here.

JOE: That's not really true, buddy, we—

HARPER: Well happy enough! Pretend-happy. That's better
than nothing.

JOE: It's time to make some changes, Harper.

HARPER: No changes. Why?

JOE: I've been chief clerk for four years. I make twenty-nine-
thousand dollars a year. That's ridiculous. I graduated
fourth in my class and I make less than anyone I know.
And I'm . . . I'm tired of being a clerk, I want to go where
something good is happening.

HARPER: Nothing good happens in Washington. We'll forget
church teachings and buy furniture at, at, Conran's and
become yuppies. I have too much to do here.

JOE: Like what?

HARPER: I *do* have things.

JOE: What things?

HARPER: I have to finish painting the bedroom.

JOE: You've been painting in there for over a year.

HARPER: I know, I— It just isn't done because I never get time
to finish it.

JOE: Oh that's . . . That doesn't make sense. You have all the
time in the world. You could finish it when I'm at work.

HARPER: I'm afraid to go in there alone.

JOE: Afraid of what?

15

HARPER: I heard someone in there. Metal scraping on the wall. A man with a knife, maybe.

JOE: There's no one in the bedroom, Harper.

HARPER: Not now.

JOE: Not this morning either.

HARPER: How do you know? You were at work this morning.
There's something creepy about this place. Remember *Rosemary's Baby*?

JOE: *Rosemary's Baby?*

HARPER: Our apartment looks like that one. Wasn't that apartment in Brooklyn?

JOE: No, it was—

HARPER: Well, it looked like this. It did.

JOE: Then let's move.

HARPER: Georgetown's worse. *The Exorcist* was in George-town.

JOE: The devil, everywhere you turn, huh, buddy.

HARPER: Yeah. Everywhere.

JOE: How many pills today, buddy?

HARPER: None. One. Three. Only three.

(At the cemetery: Rabbi Isidor Chemelwitz, heading home, walks past Louis, who is still staring into the grave. Louis stops the Rabbi with a question.)

LOUIS: Why are there just two little wooden pegs holding the lid down?

RABBI ISIDOR CHEMELWITZ: So she can get out easier if she wants to.

LOUIS: I hope she stays put.
I pretended for years that she was already dead. When they called to say she had died it was a surprise. I abandoned her.

RABBI ISIDOR CHEMELWITZ: "Sharfer vi di tson fun a shlang iz an umdankbar kind!"

LOUIS: I don't speak Yiddish.

RABBI ISIDOR CHEMELWITZ: "Sharper than the serpent's tooth is the ingratitude of children." Shakespeare. *Kenig Lear.*

LOUIS: Rabbi, what does the Holy Writ say about someone who abandons someone he loves at a time of great need?

RABBI ISIDOR CHEMELWITZ: Why would a person do such a thing?

LOUIS: Because he has to.

Maybe because this person's sense of the world, that it will change for the better with struggle, maybe a person who has this neo-Hegelian positivist sense of constant historical progress towards happiness or perfection or something, who feels very powerful because he feels connected to these forces, moving uphill all the time . . . Maybe that person can't, um, incorporate sickness into his sense of how things are supposed to go. Maybe vomit . . . and sores and disease . . . really frighten him, maybe . . . he isn't so good with death.

RABBI ISIDOR CHEMELWITZ: The Holy Scriptures have nothing to say about such a person.

LOUIS: Rabbi, I'm afraid of the crimes I may commit.

RABBI ISIDOR CHEMELWITZ: Please, mister. I'm a sick old rabbi facing a long drive home to the Bronx. You want to confess, better you should find a priest.

LOUIS: But I'm not a Catholic, I'm a Jew.

RABBI ISIDOR CHEMELWITZ: Worse luck for you, bubbulah. Catholics believe in Forgiveness. Jews believe in Guilt.

(The Rabbi turns to leave.)

LOUIS: You just make sure those pegs are in good and tight.

(The Rabbi stops, looks down into the grave, then at Louis:)

RABBI ISIDOR CHEMELWITZ: Don't worry, mister. The life she had, she'll stay put. She's better off.

(The Rabbi exits. Louis looks into the grave, one last, quick glance, then follows.)

JOE: Look, I know this is scary for you. But try to understand what it means to me. Will you try?

HARPER: Yes.

JOE: Good. Really try.

I think things are starting to change in the world.

HARPER: But I don't want—

JOE: Wait. For the good. Change for the good. America has rediscovered itself. Its sacred position among nations. And people aren't ashamed of that like they used to be. This is a great thing. The truth restored. Law restored. That's what President Reagan's done, Harper. He says: "Truth exists and can be spoken proudly." And the country responds to him. We become better. More good. I need to be a part of that, I need something big to lift me up. I mean, six years ago the world seemed in decline, horrible, hopeless, full of unsolvable problems and crime and confusion and hunger and—

HARPER: But it still seems that way. More now than before. They say the ozone layer is—

JOE: Harper . . .

HARPER: And today out the window on Atlantic Avenue there was a schizophrenic traffic cop who was making these—

JOE: Stop it! I'm trying to make a point.

HARPER: So am I.

JOE: You aren't even making sense, you—

HARPER: My point is the world seems just as—

JOE: It only seems that way to you because you never go out in the world, Harper, and you have emotional problems.

HARPER: I do so get out in the world.

JOE: You don't. You stay in all day, fretting about imaginary—

HARPER: I get out. I do. You don't know what I do.

JOE: You don't stay in all day.

HARPER: No.

JOE: Well . . . Yes you do.

HARPER: That's what you think.

JOE: Where do you go?

HARPER: Where do *you* go? When you walk.

(*Pause, then very angry*) And I DO NOT have emotional problems.

JOE: I'm sorry.

HARPER: And if I do have emotional problems it's from living with you. Or—

JOE: I'm sorry, buddy, I didn't mean to—

HARPER: Or if you do think I do then you should never have married me. You have all these secrets and lies.

JOE: I want to be married to you, Harper.

HARPER: You shouldn't. You never should.

(*Pause*)

Hey, buddy. Hey, buddy.

JOE: Buddy kiss.

(*They kiss.*)

HARPER: I heard on the radio how to give a blowjob.

JOE: What?

HARPER: You want to try?

JOE: You really shouldn't listen to stuff like that.

HARPER: Mormons can give blowjobs.

JOE: *Harper.*

HARPER *(Imitating his tone)*: *Joe.*

It was a little Jewish lady with a German accent. This is a good time. For me to make a baby.

(Little pause. Joe turns away from her, then leaves the living room.)

HARPER: Then they went on to a program about holes in the ozone layer. Over Antarctica. Skin burns, birds go blind, icebergs melt. The world's coming to an end.

Scene 6

First week of November. In the men's room of the offices of the Brooklyn Federal Court of Appeals. Louis is crying over the sink; Joe enters.

JOE: Oh, um . . . Morning.

LOUIS: Good morning, Counselor.

JOE *(He watches Louis cry)*: Sorry, I . . . I don't know your name.

LOUIS: Don't bother. Word processor. The lowest of the low.

JOE *(Holding out his hand)*: Joe Pitt. I'm with Justice Wilson.

LOUIS: Oh, I know that. Counselor Pitt. Chief Clerk.

JOE: Were you . . . Are you OK?

LOUIS: Oh, yeah. Thanks. What a nice man.

JOE: Not so nice.

LOUIS: What?

JOE: Not so nice. Nothing. You sure you're—

LOUIS: Life sucks shit. Life . . . just sucks shit.

JOE: What's wrong?

LOUIS: Run in my nylons.

JOE: Sorry . . . ?

LOUIS: Forget it. Look, thanks for asking.

JOE: Well . . .

LOUIS: I mean it really is nice of you.

> *(He starts crying again)*
>
> Sorry, sorry. Sick friend . . .

JOE: Oh, I'm sorry.

LOUIS: Yeah, yeah, well, that's sweet.

> Three of your colleagues have preceded you to this baleful sight and you're the first one to ask. The others just opened the door, saw me, and fled. I hope they had to pee real bad.

JOE *(Handing him a wad of toilet paper)*: They just didn't want to intrude.

LOUIS: Hah. Reaganite heartless macho asshole lawyers.

JOE: Oh, that's unfair.

LOUIS: What is? Heartless? Macho? Reaganite? Lawyer?

JOE: I voted for Reagan.

LOUIS: You did?

JOE: Twice.

LOUIS: Twice? Well, oh boy. A Gay Republican.

JOE: Excuse me?

LOUIS: Nothing.

JOE: I'm not—

> Forget it.

LOUIS: Republican? Not Republican? Or . . .

JOE: What?

LOUIS: What?

JOE: Not gay. I'm not gay.

LOUIS: Oh. Sorry.

> *(Blows his nose loudly)* It's just—

JOE: Yes?

LOUIS: Well, sometimes you can tell from the way a person sounds, that— I mean you *sound* like a—

JOE: No I don't.

Like what?

LOUIS: Like a Republican.

(Little pause. Joe knows he's being teased; Louis knows he knows. Joe decides to be a little brave.)

JOE: Do I? Sound like a . . . ?

LOUIS: What? Like a . . . ? Republican, or . . . ?

Do I?

JOE: Do you what?

LOUIS: Sound like a . . . ?

JOE: Like a . . . ?

I'm . . . confused.

LOUIS: Yes.

My name is Louis. But all my friends call me Louise. I work in Word Processing. Thanks for the toilet paper.

(Louis offers Joe his hand. Joe reaches, Louis feints and pecks Joe on the cheek, then exits.)

Scene 7

A week later. Mutual dream scene. Prior is dreaming that he's at a fantastic makeup table, applying his face. Harper is having a pill-induced hallucination. She has these from time to time. For some reason, Prior has appeared in this one. Or Harper has appeared in Prior's dream. It is bewildering.

PRIOR *(His makeup complete, he examines its perfection in the mirror; then he turns to the audience)*: I'm ready for my closeup, Mr. DeMille.

One wants to move through life with elegance and grace, blossoming infrequently but with exquisite taste, and perfect timing, like a rare bloom, a zebra orchid . . . One wants . . .

But one so seldom gets what one wants, does one?

No. One does not. *(Sorrow and anger well up, overwhelming the grand manner)* One gets fucked. Over. One . . . dies at thirty, robbed of . . . decades of majesty . . .

(Angry) Fuck this shit. Fuck this shit.

(He consults the mirror, attempting to resume the pose)

I look like a corpse. A . . . *corpsette!*

(It doesn't work. Commiserating with his reflection)

Oh my queen; you know you've hit rock-bottom when even drag is a drag.

(Harper appears. Prior is surprised!)

HARPER: Are you . . . Who are you?

PRIOR: Who are you?

HARPER: What are you doing in my hallucination?

PRIOR: I'm not in your hallucination. You're in my dream.

HARPER: You're wearing makeup.

PRIOR: So are you.

HARPER: But you're a man.

PRIOR *(He looks in his mirror, SCREAMS!, mimes slashing his throat with his lipstick and dies, fabulously tragic. Then)*: The hands and feet give it away.

HARPER: There must be some mistake here. I don't recognize you. You're not— Are you my . . . some sort of imaginary friend?

PRIOR: No. Aren't you too old to have imaginary friends?

HARPER: I have emotional problems. I took too many pills. Why are you wearing makeup?

PRIOR: I was in the process of applying the face, trying to make myself feel better—I swiped the new fall colors at the Clinique counter at Macy's.

(He shows her.)

HARPER: You stole these?

PRIOR: I was out of cash; it was an emotional emergency!

HARPER: Joe will be so angry. I promised him. No more pills.

PRIOR: These pills you keep alluding to?

HARPER: Valium. I take Valium. Lots of Valium.

PRIOR: And you're dancing as fast as you can.

HARPER: I'm not *addicted*. I don't believe in addiction, and I never— Well, I *never* drink. And I *never* take drugs.

PRIOR: Well, smell *you*, Nancy Drew.

HARPER: Except Valium.

PRIOR: Except Valium; in wee fistfuls.

HARPER: It's terrible. Mormons are not supposed to be addicted to anything. I'm a Mormon.

PRIOR: I'm a homosexual.

HARPER: Oh! In my church we don't believe in homosexuals.

PRIOR: In my church we don't believe in Mormons.

HARPER: What church do . . . Oh! *(She laughs)* I get it.

I don't understand this. If I didn't ever see you before and I don't think I did, then I don't think you should be here, in this hallucination, because in my experience the mind, which is where hallucinations come from, shouldn't be able to make up anything that wasn't there to start with, that didn't enter it from experience, from the real world. Imagination can't create anything new, can it? It only recycles bits and pieces from the world and reassembles them into visions . . . Am I making sense right now?

PRIOR: Given the circumstances, yes.

HARPER: So when we think we've escaped the unbearable ordinariness and, well, untruthfulness of our lives, it's really only the same old ordinariness and falseness rearranged into the appearance of novelty and truth. Nothing unknown is knowable. Don't you think it's depressing?

PRIOR: The limitations of the imagination?

HARPER: Yes.

PRIOR: It's something you learn after your second theme party: It's All Been Done Before.

HARPER: The world. Finite. Terribly, terribly . . . Well . . .
This is the most depressing hallucination I've ever had.

PRIOR: Apologies. I do try to be amusing.

HARPER: Oh, well, don't apologize, you . . . I can't expect someone who's really sick to entertain me.

PRIOR: How on earth did you know . . . ?

HARPER: Oh that happens. This is the very threshold of revelation sometimes. You can see things . . . how sick you are. Do you see anything about me?

PRIOR: Yes.

HARPER: What?

PRIOR: You are amazingly unhappy.

HARPER: Oh big deal. You meet a Valium addict and you figure out she's unhappy. That doesn't count. Of course I . . . Something else. Something surprising.

PRIOR: Something surprising.

HARPER: Yes.

PRIOR: Your husband's a homo.

(Pause.)

HARPER: Oh, ridiculous.
> *(Pause, then very quietly:)*
> Really?

PRIOR *(Shrugs)*: Threshold of revelation.

HARPER: Well I don't like your revelations. I don't think you intuit well at all. Joe's a very normal man, he . . .
> Oh God. Oh God. He . . . Do homos take, like, lots of long walks?

PRIOR *(A beat, then)*: Yes. We do. In stretch pants with lavender coifs. Up and down the avenues of Sodom we walk. Doomed, doomed...
> I just looked at you, and there was . . .

HARPER: A sort of blue streak of recognition.

PRIOR: Yes.

HARPER: Like you knew me incredibly well.

PRIOR: Yes.

HARPER: Yes.
> I have to go now, get back, something just . . . fell apart.
> Oh God, I feel so sad . . .

PRIOR: I . . . I'm sorry. I usually say, "Fuck the truth," but mostly, the truth fucks you.

HARPER: I see something else about you.

PRIOR: Oh?

HARPER: Deep inside you, there's a part of you, the most inner part, entirely free of disease. I can see that.

PRIOR: Is that— That isn't true.

HARPER: Threshold of revelation.
> Home . . .

(She vanishes. Prior's startled. Then he feels very alone.)

PRIOR: People come and go so quickly here . . .
> I don't think there's any uninfected part of me. My heart is pumping polluted blood. I feel dirty.

(He starts to wipe off his makeup; suddenly, he smears it furiously around.

A large gray feather falls from above. Prior stops smearing the makeup and looks at the feather. He goes to it and picks it up.)

A VOICE *(It is an incredibly beautiful voice)*: Look up!
PRIOR *(Looking up, not seeing anyone)*: Hello?
A VOICE: Look up!
PRIOR: Who is that?
A VOICE: Prepare the way!
PRIOR: I don't see any—

(There is a dramatic change in lighting, from above.)

A VOICE: Look up, look up,
    prepare the way
    the infinite descent
    A breath in air
    floating down
    Glory to . . .

(Silence.)

PRIOR: Hello? Is that it? Helloooo!
    (Very frightened) What the fuck? . . . *(He holds himself)*
    Poor me. Poor poor me. Why me? Why poor poor me?
    Oh I don't feel good right now. I really don't.

Scene 8

That night. Split scene: Prior and Louis in their bed. Louis reading, Prior cuddled next to him. Harper in Brooklyn, alone. Joe enters.

HARPER: Where were you?

JOE: Out.

HARPER: Where?

JOE: Just out. Thinking.

HARPER: It's late.

JOE: I had a lot to think about.

HARPER: I burned dinner.

JOE: Sorry.

HARPER: Not my dinner. My dinner was fine. Your dinner. I put it back in the oven and turned everything up as high as it could go and I watched till it burned black. It's still hot. Very hot. Want it?

JOE: You didn't have to do that.

HARPER: I know. It just seemed like the kind of thing a mentally deranged sex-starved pill-popping housewife would do.

JOE: Uh-huh.

HARPER: So I did it. Who knows anymore what I have to do?

JOE: How many pills?

HARPER: A bunch. Don't change the subject.

JOE: I won't talk to you when you—

HARPER: No. No. Don't do that! I'm . . . I'm fine, pills are not the problem, not our problem. I WANT TO KNOW WHERE YOU'VE BEEN! I WANT TO KNOW WHAT'S GOING ON!

JOE: Going on with what? The job?

HARPER: Not the job.

JOE: I said I need more time.

HARPER: Not the job!

JOE: Mr. Cohn, I talked to him on the phone, he said I had to hurry—

HARPER: Not the—

JOE: But I can't get you to talk sensibly about anything so—

HARPER: SHUT UP!

JOE: Then what?

HARPER: Stick to the subject.

JOE: I don't know what that is. You have something you want to ask me? Ask me. Go.

HARPER: I . . . can't. I'm scared of you.

JOE: I'm tired, I'm going to bed.

HARPER: Tell me without making me ask. Please.

JOE: This is crazy, I'm not—

HARPER: When you come through the door at night your face is never exactly the way I remembered it. I get surprised by something . . . mean and hard about the way you look. Even the weight of you in the bed at night, the way you breathe in your sleep seems unfamiliar.

You terrify me.

JOE: I know who you are.

HARPER: Yes. I'm the enemy. That's easy. That doesn't change.

You think you're the only one who hates sex; I do; I hate it with you; I do. I dream that you batter away at me till all my joints come apart, like wax, and I fall into pieces. It's like a punishment. It was wrong of me to marry you. I knew you—

(She stops herself)

It's a sin, and it's killing us both.

JOE: I can always tell when you've taken pills because it makes you red-faced and sweaty and frankly that's very often why I don't want to . . .

HARPER: Because . . .

JOE: Well you aren't pretty. Not like this.

HARPER: I have something to ask you.

JOE: Then ASK! ASK! What in hell are you—

HARPER: *Are you a homo?*

(*Pause*)

Are you?

If you try to walk out right now I'll put your dinner back in the oven and turn it up so high the whole building will fill with smoke and everyone in it will asphyxiate. So help me God I will.

Now answer the question.

JOE: What if I . . .

(*Small pause.*)

HARPER: Then tell me, please. And we'll scc.

JOE: No. I'm not.

I don't see what difference it makes.

(*Louis and Prior are lying on the bed, Prior's head resting on Louis's chest.*)

LOUIS: Jews don't have any clear textual guide to the afterlife; even that it exists. I don't think much about it. I see it as a perpetual rainy Thursday afternoon in March. Dead leaves.

PRIOR: Eeeugh. Very Greco-Roman.

LOUIS: Well for us it's not the verdict that counts, it's the act of judgment. That's why I could never be a lawyer. In court all that matters is the verdict.

PRIOR: You could never be a lawyer because you are oversexed. You're too distracted.

LOUIS: Not distracted; *ab*stracted. I'm trying to make a point:

PRIOR: Namely:

LOUIS: It's the judge in his or her chambers, weighing, books open, pondering the evidence, ranging freely over categories: good, evil, innocent, guilty; the judge in the chamber of circumspection, not the judge on the bench with the gavel. The shaping of the law, not its execution.

PRIOR: The point, dear, the point . . .

LOUIS: That it should be the questions and shape of a life, its total complexity gathered, arranged and considered, which matters in the end, not some stamp of salvation or damnation which disperses all the complexity in some unsatisfying little decision—the balancing of the scales . . .

PRIOR: I like this; very zen; it's . . . reassuringly incomprehensible and useless. We who are about to die thank you.

LOUIS: You are not about to die.

PRIOR: It's not going well, really . . . Two new lesions. My leg hurts. There's protein in my urine, the doctor says, but who knows what the fuck that portends. Anyway it shouldn't be there, the protein. My butt is chapped from diarrhea and yesterday I shat blood.

LOUIS: I really hate this. You don't tell me—

PRIOR: You get too upset, I wind up comforting you. It's easier—

LOUIS: Oh thanks.

PRIOR: If it's bad I'll tell you.

LOUIS: Shitting blood sounds bad to me.

PRIOR: And I'm telling you.

LOUIS: And I'm handling it.

PRIOR: Tell me some more about justice.

LOUIS: I *am* handling it.

PRIOR: Well Louis you win Trooper of the Month.

(Louis starts to cry.)

PRIOR: I take it back. You aren't Trooper of the Month.
This isn't working.
Tell me some more about justice.

LOUIS: You are not about to die.

PRIOR: Justice . . .

LOUIS: . . . is an immensity, a . . . confusing vastness.
Justice is God.
(Little pause)
Prior?

PRIOR: Hmmm?

LOUIS: You love me.

PRIOR: Yes.

LOUIS: What if I walked out on this?
Would you hate me forever?

(Prior kisses Louis on the forehead.)

PRIOR: Yes.

(Prior sits at the foot of the bed, facing out, away from Louis.)

JOE: I think we ought to pray. Ask God for help. Ask him together.

HARPER: God won't talk to me. I have to make up people to talk to me.

JOE: You have to keep asking.

HARPER: I forgot the question.
Oh yeah. God, is my husband a—

JOE *(Scary)*: Stop it. Stop it. I'm warning you.
Does it make any difference? That I might be one thing deep within, no matter how wrong or ugly that thing is, so long as I have fought, with everything I have, to kill it. What do you want from me? What do you want from me,

Harper? More than that? For God's sake, there's nothing left, I'm a shell. There's nothing left to kill.

As long as my behavior is what I know it has to be. Decent. Correct. That alone in the eyes of God.

HARPER: No, no, not that, that's Utah talk, Mormon talk, I hate it, Joe, tell me, say it.

JOE: All I will say is that I am a very good man who has worked very hard to become good and you want to destroy that. You want to destroy me, but I am not going to let you do that.

(Little pause.)

HARPER: I'm going to have a baby.

JOE: Liar.

HARPER: You liar.

⌈A baby born addicted to pills. A baby who does not dream but who hallucinates, who stares up at us with big mirror eyes and who does not know who we are.⌋

(Pause.)

JOE: Are you really . . . ?

HARPER: No.

(He turns to go.)

HARPER: Yes.

(He stops. He believes her.)

HARPER: No.
Yes.

33

(He tries to approach her.)

HARPER: Get away from me.
　　Now we both have a secret.

(Joe leaves the room.)

PRIOR *(Speaking to Louis but not looking at him)*: One of my
　　ancestors was a ship's captain who made money bringing
　　whale oil to Europe and returning with immigrants—
　　Irish mostly, packed in tight, so many dollars per head.
　　The last ship he captained foundered off the coast of
　　Nova Scotia in a winter tempest and sank to the bottom.
　　He went down with the ship—*La Grande Geste*—but
　　his crew took seventy women and kids in the ship's only
　　longboat, this big, open rowboat, and when the weather
　　got too rough, and they thought the boat was overcrowd-
　　ed, the crew started lifting people up and hurling them
　　into the sea. Until they got the ballast right. They walked
　　up and down the longboat, eyes to the waterline, and
　　when the boat rode low in the water they'd grab the near-
　　est passenger and throw them into the sea. The boat was
　　leaky, see; seventy people; they arrived in Halifax with
　　nine people on board.
LOUIS: Jesus.
PRIOR: I think about that story a lot now. People in a boat,
　　waiting, terrified, while implacable, unsmiling men, irre-
　　sistibly strong, seize . . . maybe the person next to you,
　　maybe you, and with no warning at all, with time only
　　for a quick intake of air you are pitched into freezing,
　　turbulent water and salt and darkness to drown.
　　　　I like your cosmology, baby. While time is running
　　out I find myself drawn to anything that's suspended,

that lacks an ending. But it seems to me that it lets you off scot-free.

LOUIS: What do you mean?

PRIOR: No judgment, no guilt or responsibility.

LOUIS: For me.

PRIOR: For anyone. It was an editorial "you."

LOUIS: Please get better. Please.

Please don't get any sicker.

Scene 9

A week later. Roy and Henry, his doctor, in Henry's office.

HENRY: Nobody knows what causes it. And nobody knows how to cure it. The best theory is that we blame a retrovirus, the Human Immunodeficiency Virus. Its presence is made known to us by the useless antibodies which appear in reaction to its entrance into the bloodstream through a cut, or an orifice. The antibodies are powerless to protect the body against it. Why, we don't know. The body's immune system ceases to function. Sometimes the body even attacks itself. At any rate it's left open to a whole horror house of infections from microbes which it usually defends against.

Like Kaposi's sarcomas. These lesions. Or your throat problem. Or the glands.

We think it may also be able to slip past the blood-brain barrier into the brain. Which is of course very bad news.

And it's fatal in we don't know what percent of people with suppressed immune responses.

(Pause. Roy sits, brooding. Henry waits. Then:)

ROY: This is very interesting, Mr. Wizard, but why the fuck are you telling me this?

HENRY *(Hesitating, confused, then)*: Well, I have just removed one of three lesions which biopsy results will probably tell us is a Kaposi's sarcoma lesion. And you have a pronounced swelling of glands in your neck, groin, and arm-pits—lymphadenopathy is another sign. And you have oral candidiasis and maybe a little more fungus under the fingernails of two digits on your right hand. So that's why—

ROY: This disease.

HENRY: Syndrome.

ROY: *Whatever.* It afflicts mostly homosexuals and drug addicts.

HENRY: Mostly. Hemophiliacs are also at risk.

ROY: Homosexuals and drug addicts. So why are you implying that I . . .

(Roy stares hard at Henry, who begins to feel nervous.)

ROY: What are you implying, Henry?

HENRY: I don't . . .

ROY: I'm not a drug addict.

HENRY: Oh come on Roy.

ROY: What, what, come on Roy what? Do you think I'm a junkie, Henry, do you see tracks?

HENRY: This is absurd.

ROY: Say it.

HENRY: Say what?

ROY: Say: "Roy Cohn, you are a . . ."

HENRY: Roy? I don't—

ROY: "You are a . . ." Go on. Not "Roy Cohn you are a drug fiend." "Roy Marcus Cohn, you are a . . ."

Go on, Henry. It starts with an "H."

HENRY: Oh I'm not going to—

ROY: *With an "H,"* Henry, and it isn't "hemophiliac." Come on . . .

HENRY: What are you doing, Roy?

ROY: No, say it. I mean it. Say: "Roy Cohn, you are a homosexual."

(With deadly seriousness)

And I will proceed, systematically, to destroy your reputation and your practice and your career in New York State, Henry. Which you know I can do.

(Pause. Henry summons his courage.)

HENRY: Roy, you have been seeing me since 1958. Apart from the facelifts I have treated you for everything from syphilis—

ROY: From a whore in Dallas.

HENRY: From syphilis to venereal warts. In your rectum. Which you may have gotten from a whore in Dallas, but it wasn't a female whore.

(A standoff. Then:)

ROY: So say it.

HENRY: Roy Cohn, you are . . .

(Roy's too scary. He tries a different approach)

You have had sex with men, many many times, Roy, and one of them, or any number of them, has made you very sick. You have AIDS.

37

ROY *(A beat, then)*: AIDS.

Your problem, Henry, is that you are hung up on
words, on labels, that you believe they mean what they
seem to mean. AIDS. Homosexual. Gay. Lesbian. You
think these are names that tell you who someone sleeps
with, but they don't tell you that.

HENRY: No?

ROY: No. Like all labels they tell you one thing and one thing
only: where does an individual so identified fit in the food
chain, in the pecking order? Not ideology, or sexual taste,
but something much simpler: clout. Not who I fuck or
who fucks me, but who will pick up the phone when
I call, who owes me favors. This is what a label refers to.
Now to someone who does not understand this, homosexual is what I am because I have sex with men. But
really this is wrong. Homosexuals are not men who sleep
with other men. Homosexuals are men who in fifteen
years of trying cannot pass a pissant antidiscrimination
bill through City Council. Homosexuals are men who
know nobody and who nobody knows. Who have zero
clout. Does this sound like me, Henry?

HENRY: No.

ROY: No. I have clout. A lot. I can pick up this phone, punch
fifteen numbers, and you know who will be on the other
end in under five minutes, Henry?

HENRY: The president.

ROY: Even better, Henry. His wife.

HENRY: I'm impressed.

ROY: I don't want you to be impressed. I want you to understand. This is not sophistry. And this is not hypocrisy.
This is reality. I have sex with men. But unlike nearly
every other man of whom this is true, I bring the guy
I'm screwing to the White House and President Reagan

smiles at us and shakes his hand. Because *what* I am is defined entirely by *who* I am. Roy Cohn is not a homosexual. Roy Cohn is a heterosexual man, Henry, who fucks around with guys.

HENRY: OK, Roy.

ROY: And what is my diagnosis, Henry?

HENRY: You have AIDS, Roy.

ROY: *No*, Henry, *no*. AIDS is what homosexuals have. I have liver cancer.

(Little pause.)

HENRY: Well, whatever the fuck you have, Roy, it's very serious, and I haven't got a damn thing for you. The NIH in Bethesda has a new drug called AZT with a two-year waiting list that not even I can get you onto. So get on the phone, Roy, and dial the fifteen numbers, and tell the First Lady you need in on an experimental treatment for liver cancer, because you can call it any damn thing you want, Roy, but what it boils down to is very bad news.

ACT TWO:

In Vitro

December 1985

Scene 1

The first week in December. Night. Prior in his underwear alone on the floor in the hallway outside his bedroom; he is much worse.

PRIOR: Louis, Louis, please wake up, oh God.

(Louis runs in.)

PRIOR: I think something horrible is wrong with me I can't breathe . . .

LOUIS *(Starting to exit)*: I'm calling the ambulance.

PRIOR: No, wait, I—

LOUIS: *Wait?* Are you fucking crazy? Oh God you're on fire, your head is on fire.

PRIOR: It hurts, it hurts . . .

LOUIS: I'm calling the ambulance.

PRIOR: I don't want to go to the hospital, I don't want to go to the hospital please let me lie here, just—

LOUIS: No, no, God, Prior, stand up—

PRIOR: DON'T TOUCH MY LEG!

LOUIS: We have to . . . Oh God this is so crazy.

PRIOR: I'll be OK if I just lie here Lou, really, if I can only sleep a little . . .

(Louis exits.)

PRIOR: Louis?

    NO! NO! Don't call, you'll send me there and I won't come back, please, please Louis I'm begging, baby, please. *(Screams) LOUIS!!*

LOUIS *(From off; hysterical)*: WILL YOU SHUT THE FUCK UP!

PRIOR *(Trying to stand)*: Aaaah. I have . . . to go to the bathroom. Wait. Wait, just— Oh. Oh God. *(He shits himself)*

LOUIS *(Entering)*: Prior? They'll be here in—

    Oh my God.

PRIOR: I'm sorry, I'm sorry.

LOUIS: What did . . . ? What?

PRIOR: I had an accident.

(Louis goes to him.)

LOUIS: This is blood.

PRIOR: Maybe you shouldn't touch it . . . me . . . I . . . *(He faints)*

LOUIS *(Quietly)*: Oh help. Oh help. Oh God oh God oh God help me I can't I can't I can't.

Scene 2

Night. Harper at home, sitting on the floor, all alone, with no lights on. We can barely see her. Joe enters, but he doesn't turn on the lights.

JOE: Why are you sitting in the dark? Turn on the light.

HARPER: *No.* I heard the sounds in the bedroom again. I know someone was in there.

JOE: No one was.

HARPER: Maybe actually in the bed, under the covers with a knife.

Oh, boy. Joe. I, um, I'm thinking of going away. By which I mean: I think I'm going off again. You . . . you know what I mean?

JOE: Please don't. Stay. We can fix it. I pray for that. This is my fault, but I can correct it. You have to try, too.

(Joe walks to a floor lamp and switches on the light, then sits next to her on the floor. As soon as he sits, Harper stands, goes to the lamp, turns off the light, and then returns to sit beside him. They sit quietly, close together, in the dark. Then:)

HARPER: When you pray, what do you pray for?

JOE: I pray for God to crush me, break me up into little pieces and start all over again.

HARPER: Oh. Please. Don't pray for that.

JOE: I had a book of Bible stories when I was a kid. There was a picture I'd look at twenty times every day: Jacob wrestles with the angel. I don't really remember the story, or why the wrestling—just the picture. Jacob is young and very strong. The angel is . . . a beautiful man, with golden hair and wings, of course. I still dream about it. Many nights.

43

I'm . . . It's me. In that struggle. Fierce, and unfair. The angel is not human, and it holds nothing back, so how could anyone human win, what kind of a fight is that? It's not just. Losing means your soul thrown down in the dust, your heart torn out from God's. But you can't not lose.

HARPER: In the whole entire world, you are the only person, the only person I love or have ever loved. And I love you terribly. Terribly. That's what's so awfully, irreducibly real. I can make up anything but I can't dream that away.

JOE: Are you . . . Are you really going to have a baby?

HARPER: It's my time, and there's no blood. I don't really know. I suppose it wouldn't be a great thing. Maybe I'm just not bleeding because I take too many pills. Maybe I'll give birth to a pill.

(He laughs a little.)

HARPER: That would give a new meaning to pill-popping, huh?

(They both laugh.)

HARPER: I think you should go to Washington. Alone. Change, like you said.

JOE: I'm not going to leave you, Harper.

HARPER *(A beat, then)*: Well maybe not. But I'm going to leave you.

Scene 3

One A.M., the next morning. A hospital room. Prior is in a bed, oxygen mask on his face, IV tubes draining bags of fluids into his veins. Emily, a nurse, finishes checking the tubes, the machines. Louis watches Emily; he avoids looking at Prior.

EMILY: He'll be all right now.

LOUIS: No he won't.

EMILY: No. I guess not. I gave him something that makes him sleep.

LOUIS: Deep asleep?

EMILY: Orbiting the moons of Jupiter.

LOUIS: A good place to be.

EMILY: Anyplace better than here. You his . . . uh . . . ?

LOUIS: Yes. I'm his uh.

EMILY: This must be hell for you.

LOUIS: It is. Hell. The After Life. Which is not at all like a rainy afternoon in March, by the way, Prior. A lot more vivid than I'd expected. Dead leaves, but the crunchy kind. Sharp, dry air. The kind of long, luxurious dying feeling that breaks your heart.

EMILY *(Not following, exactly)*: Yeah, well. We all get to break our hearts on this one.

He seems like a nice guy. Cute.

LOUIS: Not like this.

Yes, he is. Was. Whatever.

EMILY: Weird name. Prior Walter. Like, "The Walter before this one."

LOUIS: Lots of Walters before this one. Prior is an old old family name in an old old family. The Walters go back to the Mayflower and beyond. Back to the Norman Conquests.

45

He says there's a Prior Walter stitched into the Bayeux tapestry.

EMILY: Is that impressive?

LOUIS: Well, it's old. Very old. Which in some circles equals impressive.

EMILY: Not in my circle. What's the name of the tapestry?

LOUIS: The Bayeux tapestry. Embroidered by La Reine Mathilde.

EMILY: I'll tell my mother. She embroiders. Drives me nuts.

LOUIS: Manual therapy for anxious hands.

EMILY: Maybe you should try it.

(Louis looks at her, then finally looks directly at Prior. Then he looks away.)

LOUIS: Mathilde stitched while William the Conqueror was off to war. She was capable of . . . more than loyalty. Devotion.

She waited for him, she stitched for years. And if he had come back broken and defeated from war, she would have loved him even more. And if he had returned mutilated, ugly, full of infection and horror, she would still have loved him; fed by pity, by a sharing of pain, she would love him even more, and even more, and she would never, never have prayed to God, please let him die if he can't return to me whole and healthy and able to live a normal life . . . If he had died, she would have buried her heart with him.

So what the fuck is the matter with me?

(Little pause)

Will he sleep through the night?

EMILY: At least.

LOUIS: I'm going.

EMILY: It's one A.M. Where do you have to go at—

LOUIS: I know what time it is. A walk. Night air, good for the . . . *(Quickly brushing his hand across his heart; then)* The park.

EMILY: Be careful.

LOUIS: Yeah. Danger.

Tell him, if he wakes up and you're still on, tell him good-bye, tell him I had to go.

Scene 4

Same night. Split scene: Joe and Roy sitting at the bar in an elegant restaurant; Louis and a Man, dressed in leather, in the Ramble in Central Park. Roy's in a tuxedo, bowtie loosened. He's been drinking heavily, a rye and soda before him. Joe's dressed casually, nursing a tumbler of club soda. Louis and the Man are eyeing each other, alternating interest and indifference.

JOE: The pills were something she started when she miscarried or . . . no, she took some before that. She had a really bad time at home, when she was a kid, her home was really bad. I think a lot of drinking and physical stuff. She doesn't talk about that, instead she talks about . . . the sky falling down, people with knives hiding under sofas. Monsters. Mormons. Everyone thinks Mormons don't come from homes like that, we aren't supposed to behave that way, but we do. It's not lying, or being two-faced. Everyone tries very hard to live up to God's strictures, which are very . . . um . . .

ROY: Strict.

JOE: I shouldn't be bothering you with this.

47

ROY: No, please. Heart to heart. Want another . . . What is that, seltzer?

JOE: The failure to measure up hits people very hard. From such a strong desire to be good they feel very far from goodness when they fail.

What scares me is that maybe what I really love in her is the part of her that's farthest from the light, from God's love; maybe I was drawn to that in the first place. And I'm keeping it alive because I need it.

ROY: Why would you need it?

JOE: There are things . . . I don't know how well we know ourselves. I mean, what if? I know I married her because she . . . because I loved it that she was always wrong, always doing something wrong, like one step out of step. In Salt Lake City that stands out. I never stood out, on the outside, but inside, it was hard for me. To pass.

ROY: Pass?

JOE: Yeah.

ROY: Pass as what?

JOE: Oh. Well . . . As someone cheerful and strong. Those who love God with an open heart unclouded by secrets and struggles are cheerful; God's easy simple love for them shows in how strong and happy they are. The saints.

ROY: But you had secrets? Secret struggles . . .

JOE: I wanted to be one of the elect, one of the Blessed. You feel you ought to be, that the blemishes are yours by choice, which of course they aren't. Harper's sorrow, that really deep sorrow, she didn't choose that. But it's there.

ROY: You didn't put it there.

JOE: No.

ROY: You sound like you think you did.

JOE: I am responsible for her.

ROY: Because she's your wife.

JOE: That. And I do love her.

ROY: Whatever. She's your wife. And so there are obligations. To her. But also to yourself.

JOE: She'd fall apart in Washington.

ROY: Then let her stay here.

JOE: She'll fall apart if I leave her.

ROY: Then bring her to Washington.

JOE: I just can't, Roy. She needs me.

ROY: Listen, Joe. I'm the best divorce lawyer in the business.

(Little pause.)

JOE: Can't Washington wait?

ROY: You do what you need to do, Joe. What *you* need. *You.* Let her life go where it wants to go. You'll both be better for that. *Somebody* should get what they want.

MAN: What do you want?

LOUIS: I want you to fuck me, hurt me, make me bleed.

MAN: I want to.

LOUIS: Yeah?

MAN: I want to hurt you.

LOUIS: Fuck me.

MAN: Yeah?

LOUIS: Hard.

MAN: Yeah? You been a bad boy?

(Pause. Louis laughs, softly.)

LOUIS: Very bad. Very bad.

MAN: You need to be punished, boy?

LOUIS: Yes. I do.

MAN: Yes what?

(Little pause.)

LOUIS: Um, I . . .

MAN: Yes *what*, boy?

LOUIS: Oh. Yes sir.

MAN: I want you to take me to your place, boy.

LOUIS: No, I can't do that.

MAN: No *what*?

LOUIS: No sir, I can't, I—
    I don't live alone, sir.

MAN: Your lover know you're out with a man tonight, boy?

LOUIS: No sir, he—
    My lover doesn't know.

MAN: Your lover know you—

LOUIS: Let's change the subject, OK? Can we go to your place?

MAN: I live with my parents.

LOUIS: Oh.

ROY: Everyone who makes it in this world makes it because
    somebody older and more powerful takes an interest. The
    most precious asset in life, I think, is the ability to be a
    good son. You have that, Joe. Somebody who can be a
    good son to a father who pushes them farther than they
    would otherwise go. I've had many fathers, I owe my life
    to them, powerful, powerful men. Walter Winchell,
    Edgar Hoover. Joe McCarthy most of all. He valued me
    because I am a good lawyer, but he loved me because
    I was and am a good son. He was a very difficult man,
    very guarded and cagey; I brought out something tender
    in him. He would have died for me. And me for him.
    Does this embarrass you?

JOE: I had a hard time with my father.

ROY: Well sometimes that's the way. Then you have to find
    other fathers, substitutes, I don't know. The father-
    son relationship is central to life. Women are for birth,
    beginning, but the father is continuance. The son offers

the father his life as a vessel for carrying forth his father's dream. Your father's living?

JOE: Um, dead.

ROY: He was . . . what? A difficult man?

JOE: He was in the military. He could be very unfair. And cold.

ROY: But he loved you.

JOE: I don't know.

ROY: No, no, Joe, he did, I know this. Sometimes a father's love has to be very, very hard, unfair even, cold to make his son grow strong in a world like this. This isn't a good world.

MAN: Here, then.

LOUIS: I . . . Do you have a rubber?

MAN: I don't use rubbers.

LOUIS: You should. *(He takes one from his coat pocket)* Here.

MAN: I don't use them.

LOUIS: Forget it, then. *(He starts to leave)*

MAN: No, wait.

Put it on me. Boy.

LOUIS: Forget it, I have to get back. Home. I must be going crazy.

MAN: Oh come on please he won't find out.

LOUIS: It's cold. Too cold.

MAN: It's never too cold, let me warm you up. Please?

(Louis puts the condom on the Man's cock, and they begin to fuck.)

MAN: Relax.

LOUIS *(A grim, small laugh)*: Not a chance.

(More fucking. It gets rough. Louis falls on his hands and knees. Then the Man stops.)

MAN: It . . .

LOUIS: What?

MAN: I think it must've . . . It broke, or slipped off, you didn't
    put it on right, or— You want me to keep going?
        Pull out? Should I—

LOUIS: Keep going.
        Infect me.
        I don't care. I don't care.

(The Man pulls out.)

MAN: I . . . um, look, I'm sorry, but I think I want to go.

LOUIS: Yeah.
        Give my best to Mom and Dad.

(The Man slaps him.)

LOUIS: Ow!

(They stare at each other.)

LOUIS: It was a joke.

(The Man leaves.)

ROY: How long have we known each other?

JOE: Since 1980.

ROY: Right. A long time. I feel close to you, Joe. Do I advise
    you well?

JOE: You've been an incredible friend, Roy, I'm—

ROY: I want to be family. *Famiglia*, as my Italian friends call it.
    La Famiglia. A lovely word. It's important for me to help
    you, like I was helped.

JOE: I owe practically everything to you, Roy.

ROY: I'm dying, Joe. Cancer.

JOE: Oh my God.

ROY: Please. Let me finish.

Few people know this and I'm telling you this only because . . . I'm not afraid of death. What can death bring that I haven't faced? I've lived; life is the worst. *(Gently mocking himself)* Listen to me, I'm a philosopher.

Joe. You must do this. You must must must. Love; that's a trap. Responsibility; that's a trap, too. Like a father to a son I tell you this: Life is full of horror; nobody escapes, nobody; save yourself. Whatever pulls on you, whatever needs from you, threatens you. Don't be afraid; people are so afraid; don't be afraid to live in the raw wind, naked, alone . . . Learn at least this: What you are capable of. Let nothing stand in your way.

Scene 5

Several days later. Prior and Belize in Prior's hospital room. Prior is very sick but improving. Belize has just arrived, stopping on his way to work to check up on Prior, with little time to spare.

PRIOR: Miss Thing.

BELIZE: Ma cherie bichette.

PRIOR: Stella.

BELIZE: Stella for star. Let me see. *(Scrutinizing Prior)* You look like shit, why yes indeed you do, comme la merde!

PRIOR: Merci.

BELIZE: Not to despair, Belle Reeve. Lookie!
     (Taking a little plastic bottle from his bag)
     Magic goop!

(Belize hands the bottle to Prior, who opens it and sniffs it suspiciously, as Belize looks over the IV bags feeding meds to Prior.)

PRIOR *(Reacting to the smell from the bottle with alarm)*: Pooh! What kinda crap is that?

BELIZE: Beats me. Let's rub it on your poor blistered body and see what it does.

PRIOR: This is not Western medicine, this bottle . . .

BELIZE: Voodoo cream. From the botanica 'round the block.

PRIOR: And you a registered nurse.

(Belize takes the bottle back and sniffs it.)

BELIZE: Beeswax and cheap perfume. Cut with Jergen's lotion. Full of good vibes and love from some little black Cubana witch in Miami.

(He pours some in his hands, ready to give Prior a backrub.)

PRIOR *(Frightened)*: Get that trash away from me, I am immune-suppressed.

BELIZE *(Firm, slightly offended)*: I *am* a health professional. I *know* what I'm doing.

(Prior hesitates, then reluctantly offers his back to be rubbed. Belize gets on the bed and rubs, gently.)

PRIOR: It stinks.

Any word from Louis?

(Little pause; Belize rubs Prior's back.)

PRIOR: Gone.

BELIZE: He'll be back. I know the type. Likes to keep a girl on edge.

PRIOR: It's been . . .

(Pause.)

BELIZE *(Trying to jog Prior's memory)*: How long?

PRIOR: I don't remember.

BELIZE: How long have you been here?

PRIOR *(Suddenly upset)*: I don't remember, I don't give a fuck. I want Louis. I want my fucking boyfriend, where the fuck is he? I'm dying, I'm dying, where's Louis?

(Prior is crying, hard. Belize cradles him.)

BELIZE: Ssssh, sssh . . .

PRIOR: This is a very strange drug, this drug. Emotional lability, for starters.

BELIZE: Save a tab or two for me.

PRIOR: Oh no, not this drug, ce n'est pas pour la joyeux noël et la bonne année, this drug she is serious poisonous chemistry, ma pauvre bichette.

And not just disorienting. I hear things.

Voices.

BELIZE *(Covering, but alarmed)*: Voices.

PRIOR: A voice.

BELIZE: Saying what?

(Pause.)

PRIOR: I'm not supposed to tell.

BELIZE *(Earnest)*: You better tell the doctor. Or I will.

55

PRIOR: No no don't. Please. I want the voice; it's wonderful. It's all that's keeping me alive. I don't want to talk to some intern about it.

　　You know what happens? When I hear it, I get hard.

BELIZE: Oh my.

PRIOR: Comme ça. *(He uses his arm to demonstrate)* And you know I am slow to rise.

BELIZE: My jaw aches at the memory.

PRIOR *(Pleading)*: And would you deny me this little solace? Betray my concupiscence to Florence Nightingale's storm troopers?

BELIZE: Perish the thought, ma bébé.

PRIOR: They'd change the drug just to spoil the fun.

BELIZE: You and your boner can depend on me.

PRIOR: Je t'adore, ma belle nègre.

BELIZE *(With an edge)*: All this girl-talk shit is politically incorrect, you know. We should have dropped it back when we gave up drag.

PRIOR *(Indignant)*: I'm sick, I get to be politically incorrect if it makes me feel better. You sound like Lou.

　　(Little pause)

　　Well, at least I have the satisfaction of knowing he's in anguish somewhere. I loved his anguish. Watching him stick his head up his asshole and eat his guts out over some relatively minor moral conundrum—it was the best show in town. But Mother warned me: if they get overwhelmed by the little things—

BELIZE: —they'll be belly-up bustville when something big comes along.

PRIOR: Mother warned me.

BELIZE: And they do come along.

PRIOR: But I didn't listen.

BELIZE: No. *(Doing Katharine Hepburn)* Men are beasts.

PRIOR *(Also Hepburn)*: The absolute lowest.

BELIZE: I have to go. If I want to spend my whole lonely life looking after white people I can get underpaid to do it.

PRIOR: You're just a Christian martyr.

BELIZE: Whatever happens, baby, I will be here for you.

PRIOR: Je t'aime.

BELIZE: Je t'aime. Don't go crazy on me, girlfriend, I already got enough crazy queens for one lifetime. For two. I can't be bothering with dementia.

PRIOR: I promise.

BELIZE *(Touching him with his forefinger; softly, doing E.T.)*: Ouch.

PRIOR: Ouch. Indeed.

BELIZE: Why'd they have to pick on you?

And eat more, girlfriend, you really do look like shit.

(He leaves.)

PRIOR *(A beat, then)*: He's gone.

Are you still—

A VOICE: I can't stay. I will return.

PRIOR: Are you one of those "Follow me to the other side" voices?

A VOICE: No. I am no nightbird. I am a messenger . . .

PRIOR: You have a beautiful voice, it sounds . . . like a viola, like a perfectly tuned, tight string, balanced, the truth . . . Stay with me.

A VOICE: Not now. Soon I will return, I will reveal myself to you; I am glorious, glorious; my heart, my countenance and my message. You must prepare.

PRIOR *(Afraid again)*: For what? I don't want to—

A VOICE: No death, no:

A marvelous work and a wonder we undertake, an edifice awry we sink plumb and straighten, a great Lie we abolish, a great error correct, with the rule, sword and broom of Truth!

PRIOR: What are you talking about, I—

A VOICE: I am on my way; when I am manifest, our Work begins:

Prepare for the parting of the air,

The breath, the ascent,

Glory to . . .

Scene 6

Several days later. Martin, a relentlessly upbeat official in the Reagan Administration's Justice Department, is at a table with Roy and Joe in a fancy Manhattan restaurant.

MARTIN: It's a revolution in Washington, Joe. We have a new agenda and finally a real leader. They got back the Senate but we have the courts. By the nineties the Supreme Court will be block-solid Republican appointees, and the federal bench—Republican judges like land mines, everywhere, everywhere they turn. Affirmative action? Take it to court. Boom! Land mine. And we'll get our way on just about everything: abortion, defense, Central America, family values, a live investment climate. We have the White House locked till the year 2000. And beyond. A permanent fix on the Oval Office? It's possible. By '92 we'll get the Senate back, and in ten years the South is going to give us the House. It's really the end of Liberalism. The end of New Deal Socialism. The end of ipso facto secular humanism. The dawning of a genuinely American political personality. Modeled on Ronald Wilson Reagan.

JOE: It sounds great, Mr. Heller.

MARTIN: Martin. And Justice is the hub. Especially since Ed Meese took over. He doesn't specialize in Fine Points of the Law. He's a flatfoot, a cop. He reminds me of Teddy Roosevelt.

JOE: I can't wait to meet him.

MARTIN: Too bad, Joe, he's been dead for sixty years!

(There is a little awkwardness. Joe doesn't respond.)

MARTIN: Teddy Roosevelt. You said you wanted to . . . Little joke. It reminds me of the story about the—

ROY *(Smiling, but nasty)*: Aw shut the fuck up, Martin.

(To Joe) You see that? Mr. Heller here is one of the mighty, Joseph, in D.C., he sitteth on the right hand of the man who sitteth on the right hand of The Man. And yet I can say "shut the fuck up" and he will take no offense. Loyalty.

MARTIN: This man, Joe, is a Saint of the Right.

JOE: I know, Mr. Heller, I—

ROY: And you see what I mean, Martin? He's special, right?

MARTIN: Don't embarrass him, Roy.

ROY: Gravity, decency, smarts! His strength is as the strength of ten because his heart is pure! *And* he's a Royboy, one hundred percent.

MARTIN: We're on the move, Joe. On the move.

JOE: Mr. Heller, I—

MARTIN: We can't wait any longer for an answer.

(Little pause.)

JOE: Oh. Um, I—

ROY: Joe's a married man, Martin.

MARTIN: Aha.

ROY: With a wife. She doesn't care to go to D.C., and so Joe cannot go. And keeps us dangling. We've seen that kind of thing before, haven't we? These men and their wives.

MARTIN: Oh yes. Beware.

JOE: I really can't discuss this under—

MARTIN: Then *don't* discuss. Say yes, Joe.

ROY: Now.

MARTIN: Say yes I will.

ROY: Now.

Now. I'll hold my breath till you do, I'm turning blue waiting . . .

(Too loud) Now, goddamnit!

MARTIN *(Looking around)*: Roy, calm down, it's not—

ROY: Aw, fuck it.

(Roy takes a letter from his jacket pocket, hands it to Joe.)

ROY: Read. Came today.

(Joe removes the letter from its envelope and reads. Then he looks up at Roy.)

JOE: Roy. This is . . . Roy, this is terrible.

ROY: You're telling me.

A letter from the New York State Bar Association, Martin.

They're gonna try and disbar me.

MARTIN: Oh my.

JOE: Why?

ROY: Why, Martin?

MARTIN: Revenge.

ROY: The whole Establishment. Their little rules. Because I know no rules. Because I don't see the Law as a dead and arbitrary collection of antiquated dictums, thou shall, thou shalt not, because, because I know the Law's a pliable, breathing, sweating . . . *organ*, because, because—

MARTIN: Because he borrowed half a million from one of his clients.

ROY: Yeah, well, there's that.

MARTIN: *And* he forgot to *return* it.

JOE: Roy, that's . . . You borrowed money from a client?

ROY: I'm deeply ashamed.

(Little pause.)

JOE: Roy, you know how much I admire you. Well I mean I know you have unorthodox ways, but I'm sure you only did what you thought at the time you needed to do. And I have faith that—

ROY: Not so damp, please. I'll deny it was a loan. She's got no paperwork. Can't prove a fucking thing.

(Little pause. Martin studies the menu.
Joe puts the letter back in its envelope and hands it to Roy.)

JOE *(A little stiff, formal)*: Roy I really appreciate your telling me this, and I'll do whatever I can to help.

ROY *(Holding up a hand, then, carefully)*: I'll tell you what you can do.

I'm about to be tried, Joe, by a jury that is not a jury of my peers. The disbarment committee: genteel gentlemen Brahmin lawyers, country-club men. I offend them, to these men I'm what, Martin? Some sort of filthy little Jewish troll?

MARTIN *(With an embarrassed laugh)*: Oh well, I wouldn't go
so far as—

ROY *(Imitating the laugh)*: Oh well I would.

Very fancy lawyers, these disbarment commit-
tee lawyers, fancy lawyers with fancy corporate clients
and complicated cases. Antitrust suits. Deregulation.
Environmental control. Complex cases like these need
Justice Department cooperation like flowers need the sun.
Wouldn't you say that's an accurate assessment, Martin?

MARTIN: I'm not here, Roy. I'm not hearing any of this.

ROY: No. Of course not.

Without the light of the sun, Joe, these cases, and the
fancy lawyers who represent them, will wither and die.

A well-placed friend, someone in the Justice Department, say, can turn off the sun. Cast a deep shadow on
my behalf. Make them shiver in the cold. If they over-
step. They would fear that.

(Pause.)

JOE: Roy. I don't understand.

ROY: You do.

(Pause.)

JOE: You're not asking me to—

ROY: Sssshhhh. Careful.

JOE *(A beat, then)*: Even if I said yes to the job, it would be
illegal to interfere. With the hearings. It's unethical. No.
I can't.

ROY: Un-ethical.

Would you excuse us, Martin?

MARTIN: Excuse you?

ROY: Take a walk, Martin. For real.

(Martin hesitates, then stands. He shoots Joe a quick "you just stepped in it" look, then leaves.)

ROY: Un-ethical. Are you trying to embarrass me in front of my friend?

JOE: Well it is unethical, I can't—

ROY: Boy, you are really something, what the fuck do you think this is, Sunday school?

JOE: No, but Roy this is—

ROY: This is—this is gastric juices churning, this is enzymes and acids, this is intestinal is what this is, bowel movement and blood-red meat! This stinks, this is *politics*, Joe, the game of being alive. And you think you're . . . What? Above that? Above alive is what? Dead! In the clouds! You're on earth, goddamnit! Plant a foot, stay a while.

    I'm sick. They smell I'm weak. They want blood this time. I must have eyes in Justice. In Justice you will protect me.

JOE: Why can't Mr. Heller—

ROY: Grow up, Joe. The administration can't get involved.

JOE: But I'd be part of the administration. The same as him.

ROY: Not the same. Martin's Ed's man. And Ed's Reagan's man. So Martin's Reagan's man.

    And you're mine.

    (Little pause. He holds up the letter)

    This will never be. Understand me?

    (He tears up the letter)

    I'm gonna be a lawyer, Joe, I'm gonna be a lawyer, Joe, I'm gonna be a goddamn motherfucking legally licensed member of the bar lawyer, just like my daddy was, till my last bitter day on earth, Joseph, until the day I die.

(Martin returns.)

ROY: Ah, Martin's back.
MARTIN: So are we agreed?
ROY: Joe?

(Little pause.)

JOE: I will think about it.
    (To Roy) I will.
ROY *(A beat, then, contemplatively)*: Huh.
MARTIN: It's the fear of what comes after the doing that makes
    the doing hard to do.
ROY: Amen.
MARTIN: But you can almost always live with the consequences.

Scene 7

That afternoon. On the granite steps outside the Hall of Justice, Brooklyn. It is cold and sunny. A Sabrett wagon is selling hot dogs. Louis, in a shabby overcoat, is sitting on the steps contemplatively eating one. Joe enters with three hot dogs and a can of Coke.

JOE: Can I . . . ?
LOUIS: Oh sure. Sure. Crazy cold sun.
JOE *(Sitting)*: Have to make the best of it.
    How's your friend?
LOUIS: My . . . ? Oh. He's worse. My friend is worse.
JOE: I'm sorry.
LOUIS: Yeah, well. Thanks for asking. It's nice. You're nice.
    I can't believe you voted for Reagan.

JOE: I hope he gets better.

LOUIS: Reagan?

JOE: Your friend.

LOUIS: He won't. Neither will Reagan.

JOE: Let's not talk politics, OK?

LOUIS *(Pointing to Joe's lunch)*: You're eating *three* of those?

JOE: Well . . . I'm . . . hungry.

LOUIS: They're really terrible for you. Full of rat poo and beetle legs and wood shavings 'n' shit.

JOE: Huh.

LOUIS: And . . . um . . . irridium, I think. Something toxic.

JOE: You're eating one.

LOUIS: Yeah, well, the shape, I can't help myself, plus I'm *trying* to commit suicide, what's your excuse?

JOE: I don't have an excuse. I just have Pepto-Bismol.

(Joe takes a bottle of Pepto-Bismol and chugs it. Louis shudders audibly.)

JOE: Yeah I know but then I wash it down with Coke.

(He does this. Louis mimes barfing in Joe's lap. Joe pushes Louis's head away.)

JOE: Are you *always* like this?

LOUIS: I've been worrying a lot about his kids.

JOE: Whose?

LOUIS: Reagan's. Maureen and Mike and little orphan Patti and Miss Ron Reagan, Jr., the you-should-pardon-the-expression heterosexual.

JOE: Ron Reagan, Jr. is *not*— You shouldn't just make these assumptions about people. How do you know? About him? What he is? You don't know.

LOUIS *(Doing Tallulah Bankhead)*: Well darling he never sucked *my* cock but—

JOE: Look, if you're going to get vulgar—

LOUIS: No no *really*, I mean, what's it like to be the child of the Zeitgeist? To have the American Animus as your dad? It's not really a *family*, the Reagans, I read *People*, there aren't any connections there, no love, they don't ever even speak to each other except through their agents. So what's it like to be Reagan's kid? Enquiring minds want to know.

JOE: You can't believe everything you—

LOUIS: But . . .

I think we all know what that's like. Nowadays. No connections. No responsibilities. All of us . . . falling through the cracks that separate what we owe to our selves and . . . and what we owe to love.

JOE *(A beat, then)*: You just . . . Whatever you feel like saying or doing, you don't care, you just . . . do it.

LOUIS *(Catching at something in Joe's tone)*: Do what?

JOE: It. Whatever. Whatever it is you want to do.

LOUIS *(A beat; then, quietly challenging)*: Are you trying to tell me something?

(Little pause, sexual. They look at each other, then Joe looks away.)

JOE: No, I'm just observing that you—

LOUIS *(Nodding, letting him off the hook)*: Impulsive.

JOE: Yes, I mean it must be scary, you—

LOUIS: Land of the free, home of the brave, call me irresponsible.

JOE: It's kind of terrifying.

LOUIS *(Shrugging)*: Yeah, well, freedom is. Heartless, too.

JOE: Oh you're not heartless.

(Little pause. Louis stops smiling.)

LOUIS: You don't know.
	Finish your weenie.

(Louis pats Joe on the knee, stands and starts to leave.)

JOE: Um . . .

(Louis turns, looks at him. Joe searches for something to say; then, mostly avoiding looking at Louis:)

JOE: Yesterday was Sunday but I've been a little unfocused recently and I thought it was Monday. So I came here like I was going to work. And the whole place was empty. And at first I couldn't figure out why, and I had this moment of incredible . . . fear and also . . . It just flashed through my mind: the whole Hall of Justice, it's empty, it's deserted, it's gone out of business. Forever. The people that make it run have up and abandoned it.

LOUIS *(Looking at the building)*: Creepy.

JOE: Well yes but. I felt that I was going to scream. Not because it was creepy, but because the emptiness felt so *fast*.
	And . . . well, good. A . . . happy scream.
	I just wondered what a thing it would be . . . if overnight everything you owe anything to, justice, or love, had really gone away. Free.
	It would be . . . heartless terror. Yes. Terrible, and . . .
	Very great. To shed your skin, every old skin, one by one and then walk away, unencumbered, into the morning.
	(Pause. He looks at the building, then down)
	I can't go in there today.

LOUIS: Then don't.

JOE: I can't go in, I need . . .

> (He looks for what he needs. He takes a swig of Pepto-Bismol)

I can't *be* this anymore. I need . . . a change, I should just . . .

LOUIS: Want some company? For whatever?

(A possibility of sex still hangs in the air.)

LOUIS: Sometimes, even if it scares you to death, you have to be willing to break the law. Know what I mean?

(Little pause.)

JOE: Yes.

LOUIS *(A beat, then)*: I moved out. I moved out on my . . .

(Little pause; Louis looks down. The sexual possibility disappears.)

LOUIS: I haven't been sleeping well.

JOE: Me neither.

(Louis licks his napkin and goes up to Joe. He dabs at Joe's upper lip.)

LOUIS: Antacid moustache.

(Louis starts to walk away, then stops and stares at the courthouse. Not looking at Joe:)

LOUIS: Maybe the court won't convene. Ever again. Maybe we are free. To do whatever.

Children of the new morning, criminal minds. Selfish and greedy and loveless and blind. Reagan's children.

(Looking at Joe) You're scared. So am I. Everybody is in the land of the free.

(Louis turns and leaves. As he's exiting:)

LOUIS: God help us all.

Scene 8

Late that night. Joe at a payphone calling Hannah at home in Salt Lake City. Joe's a little drunk.

JOE: Mom?

HANNAH: Joe?

JOE: Hi.

HANNAH: You're calling from the street. It's . . . it must be four in the morning. What's happened?

JOE: Nothing, nothing, I—

HANNAH: It's Harper. Is Harper—

    Joe?

    Joe?

JOE: Yeah, hi. No, Harper's fine. Well, no, she's . . . *(He finds this slightly funny)* not fine.

    (With a grin) How are you, Mom?

HANNAH: What's happened?

JOE: I just wanted to talk to you. I, uh, wanted to try something out on you.

HANNAH: Joe, you haven't— Have you been drinking, Joe?

JOE *(A bigger grin)*: Yes, ma'am. I'm drunk.

HANNAH: That isn't like you.

JOE: No. I mean— *(Again, finding this a little funny)* Who's to say?

HANNAH: Why are you out on the street at four A.M.? In that crazy city. It's dangerous.

JOE: Actually, Mom, I'm not on the street. I'm near the boathouse in the park.

HANNAH: What park?

JOE: Central Park.

HANNAH: CENTRAL PARK! Oh my Lord. What on earth are you doing in Central Park at this time of night? Are you—

(Very stern) Joe, I think you ought to go home right now. Call me from home.

(Little pause.)

HANNAH: Joe?

JOE: I come here to watch, Mom. Sometimes. Just to watch.

HANNAH: Watch what? What's there to watch at four in the—

JOE: Mom, did Dad love me?

HANNAH: What?

JOE: Did he?

HANNAH: You ought to go home and call from there.

JOE: Answer.

HANNAH: Oh now really. This is maudlin. I don't like this conversation.

JOE: Yeah, well, it gets worse from here on.

(Pause.)

HANNAH: Joe?

JOE: Mom. Momma. I'm a homosexual, Momma.
   (He lowers the receiver and laughs quietly to himself)
   Boy, did that come out awkward.
   (He lifts the receiver to his ear)
   Hello? Hello?
   I'm a homosexual.
   (Pause)
   Please, Momma. Say something.

HANNAH: You're old enough to understand that your father
   didn't love you without being ridiculous about it.

JOE: What?

HANNAH: You're ridiculous. You're being ridiculous.

JOE: I'm— *What?*

HANNAH: You really ought to go home now to your wife.
   I need to go to bed. This phone call— We will just forget
   this phone call.

JOE: Mom.

HANNAH: No more talk. Tonight. This . . .
   (Suddenly very angry) Drinking is a sin! A sin! I raised
   you better than that. *(She hangs up)*

Scene 9

The following morning, early. Split scene: Harper and Joe at home; Louis and Prior in Prior's hospital room. Joe and Louis have each just entered. This should be fast. No freezing; even when one of the couples isn't talking, they remain furiously alive.

HARPER: Oh God. Home. The moment of truth has arrived.

JOE: Harper.

LOUIS: I'm going to move out.

PRIOR: The fuck you are.

JOE: Harper. Please listen. I still love you very much. You're still my best buddy; I'm not going to leave you.

HARPER: No, I don't like the sound of this. I'm leaving.

LOUIS: I'm leaving.

I already have.

JOE: Please listen. Stay. This is really hard. We have to talk.

HARPER: We are talking. Aren't we. Now please shut up. OK?

PRIOR: Bastard. Sneaking off while I'm flat out here, that's low.

If I could get up now I'd beat the holy shit out of you.

JOE: Did you take pills? How many?

HARPER: No pills. Bad for the . . . *(Pats stomach)*

JOE: You aren't pregnant. I called your gynecologist.

HARPER: I'm seeing a new gynecologist.

PRIOR: You have no right to do this.

LOUIS: Oh, that's ridiculous.

PRIOR: No right. It's criminal.

JOE: Forget about that. Just listen. You want the truth. This is the truth.

I knew this when I married you. I've known this I guess for as long as I've known anything, but . . . I don't know, I thought maybe that with enough effort and will I could change myself . . . but I can't . . .

PRIOR: Criminal.

LOUIS: There oughta be a law.

PRIOR: There is a law. You'll see.

JOE: I'm losing ground here, I go walking, you want to know where I walk, I . . . go to the park, or up and down 53rd Street, or places where . . . And I keep swearing I won't go walking again, but I just can't.

LOUIS: I need some privacy.

PRIOR: That's new.

LOUIS: Everything's new, Prior.

JOE: I try to tighten my heart into a knot, a snarl, I try to learn to live dead, just numb, but then I see someone I want, and it's like a nail, like a hot spike right through my chest, and I know I'm losing.

PRIOR: Apartment too small for three? Louis and Prior comfy but not Louis and Prior and Prior's disease?

LOUIS: Something like that.

I won't be judged by you. This isn't a crime, just—the inevitable consequence of people who run out of—whose limitations—

PRIOR: Bang bang bang. The court will come to order.

LOUIS: I mean let's talk practicalities, schedules; I'll come over if you want, spend nights with you when I can, I can—

PRIOR: Has the jury reached a verdict?

LOUIS: I'm doing the best I can.

PRIOR: Pathetic. Who cares?

JOE: My whole life has conspired to bring me to this place, and I can't despise my whole life. I think I believed when I met you I could save you, you at least if not myself, but . . .

I don't have any sexual feelings for you, Harper. And I don't think I ever did.

(Little pause.)

HARPER: I think you should go.

JOE: Where?

HARPER: Washington. Doesn't matter.

JOE: What are you talking about?

HARPER: Without me.

Without me, Joe. Isn't that what you want to hear?

(Little pause.)

JOE: Yes.

LOUIS: You can love someone and fail them. You can love someone and not be able to—

PRIOR: You *can*, theoretically, yes. A person can, maybe an editorial "you" can love, Louis, but not *you*, specifically you. I don't know, I think you are excluded from that general category.

HARPER: You were going to save me, but the whole time you were spinning a lie. I just don't understand that.

PRIOR: A person could theoretically love and maybe many do but we both know now you can't.

LOUIS: I do.

PRIOR: You can't even say it.

LOUIS: I love you, Prior.

PRIOR: I repeat. Who cares?

HARPER: This is so scary, I want this to stop, to go back.

PRIOR: We have reached a verdict, Your Honor. This man's heart is deficient. He loves, but his love is worth nothing.

JOE: Harper . . .

HARPER: Mr. Lies, I want to get away from here. Far away. Right now. Before he starts talking again. Please, please—

JOE: As long as I've known you Harper you've been afraid of . . . of men hiding under the bed, men hiding under the sofa, men with knives.

PRIOR *(Shattered; almost pleading; trying to reach him)*: I'm dying! You stupid fuck! Do you know what that is! Love! Do you know what love means? We lived together four and a half years, you animal, you idiot.

LOUIS: I have to find some way to save myself.

JOE: Who are these men? I never understood it. Now I know.

HARPER: What?

JOE: It's me.

HARPER: It is?

PRIOR: Get out of my room.

JOE: I'm the man with the knives.

HARPER: You are?

PRIOR: If I could get up now I'd kill you. I would. Go away.
Go away or I'll scream.

HARPER: Oh God . . .

JOE: I'm sorry.

HARPER: It is you.

LOUIS: Please don't scream.

PRIOR: Go.

HARPER: I recognize you now.

LOUIS: Please . . .

JOE: Oh. Wait, I . . . Oh!

> *(He covers his mouth with his hand, gags, and removes his
> hand, red with blood)*
>
> I'm bleeding.

(Prior closes his eyes and screams.)

HARPER: Mr. Lies.

MR. LIES *(Appearing, dressed in Antarctic explorer's apparel)*: Right
here.

HARPER: I want to go away. I can't see him anymore.

MR. LIES: Where?

HARPER: Anywhere. Far away.

MR. LIES: Absolutamento.

(Harper and Mr. Lies vanish. Joe looks up, sees that she's gone.)

PRIOR: When I open my eyes you'll be gone.

(Louis leaves.)

JOE: Harper?
PRIOR *(Opening his eyes)*: Huh. It worked.
JOE *(Calling)*: *Harper?*
PRIOR: I hurt all over. I wish I was dead.

Scene 10

The same day, sunset, in front of Hannah's house in Salt Lake City. Hannah and Sister Ella Chapter, a real-estate saleswoman and Hannah Pitt's closest friend—although Hannah is never friendly and Ella is severely intimidated by her.

SISTER ELLA CHAPTER: Look at that view! A view of Heaven. Like the living city of Heaven, isn't it, it just fairly glimmers in the sun.
HANNAH: Glimmers.
SISTER ELLA CHAPTER: Even the stone and brick it just glimmers and glitters like Heaven in the sunshine. Such a nice view you get, perched up on a canyon rim. Some kind of beautiful place.
HANNAH: It's just Salt Lake, and you're selling the house *for* me, not *to* me.
SISTER ELLA CHAPTER: I like to work up an enthusiasm for my properties.
HANNAH: Just get me a good price.
SISTER ELLA CHAPTER: Well, the market's off.
HANNAH: At least fifty.
SISTER ELLA CHAPTER: Forty'd be more like it.
HANNAH: Fifty.

SISTER ELLA CHAPTER: Wish you'd wait a bit.

HANNAH: Well I can't.

SISTER ELLA CHAPTER: Wish you would. You're about the only friend I got.

HANNAH: Oh well now.

SISTER ELLA CHAPTER: Know why I decided to like you? I decided to like you 'cause you're the only unfriendly Mormon I ever met.

HANNAH: Your wig is crooked.

SISTER ELLA CHAPTER: Fix it.

(Hannah straightens Ella's wig.)

SISTER ELLA CHAPTER: New York City. All they got there is tiny rooms.

I always thought: People ought to stay put. That's why I got my license to sell real estate. It's a way of saying: Have a house! Stay put! It's a way of saying traveling's no good. Plus I needed the cash.

(She takes out a pack of cigarettes from her purse, lights one, offers the pack to Hannah.)

HANNAH: Not out here, anyone could come by.

(Ella smokes. Hannah looks out over the ledge.)

HANNAH: There's been days I've stood at this ledge and thought about stepping over.

(This is news to Ella.)

HANNAH: It's a hard place, Salt Lake: baked dry. Abundant energy; not much intelligence. That's a combination that

77

can wear a body out. No harm looking someplace else. I don't need much room.

My sister-in-law Libby thinks there's radon gas in the basement.

SISTER ELLA CHAPTER *(Immediately alarmed)*: Is there gas in the—

HANNAH: Of course not. Libby's a fool.

SISTER ELLA CHAPTER *(Still alarmed)*: 'Cause I'd have to include that in the description.

HANNAH *(Ending it)*: There's no gas, Ella.

(Little pause, then) Give a puff.

(Hannah takes a furtive drag of Ella's cigarette. Then she hands the cigarette back to Ella.)

HANNAH: Put it away now.

(Ella carefully knocks the ash off the cigarette, extinguishes it and returns it to the pack. Desolate, she looks at Hannah.)

SISTER ELLA CHAPTER: So I guess it's good-bye.

HANNAH *(Uncomfortable)*: You'll be all right, Ella, I wasn't ever much of a friend.

SISTER ELLA CHAPTER: I'll say something but don't laugh, OK?

(Tentative, careful) This is the home of saints, the god-liest place on earth, they say, and I think they're right. That mean there's no evil here? No. Evil's everywhere. Sin's everywhere. But this . . . is the spring of sweet water in the desert, the desert flower. Every step a Believer takes away from here is a step fraught with peril. I fear for you, Hannah Pitt, because you are my friend. Stay put. This is the right home of saints.

HANNAH: Latter-day saints.

SISTER ELLA CHAPTER: Only kind left.

HANNAH: But still. Late in the day . . . for saints and everyone. That's all. That's all.

Fifty thousand dollars for the house, Sister Ella Chapter; don't undersell. It's an impressive view.

ACT THREE:

Not-Yet-Conscious,
Forward Dawning

December 1985

Scene 1

Late night, several days after the end of Act Two. Prior's bedroom,
completely dark. Prior is in bed, having a nightmare. He wakes up,
sits up in bed, and switches on a lamp. He looks at his clock. Seated
by the table near the bed is a man, fierce and gloomy, dressed in the
clothing of a thirteenth-century British farmer/squire, carrying a
scythe. Prior is terrified.

PRIOR: Who are you?!
PRIOR 1: My name is Prior Walter.

    (Little pause.)

PRIOR: My name is Prior Walter.

PRIOR 1: I know that.

PRIOR: Explain.

PRIOR 1: You're alive. I'm not. We have the same name. What do you want me to explain?

PRIOR: A ghost?

PRIOR 1: An ancestor.

PRIOR: Not *the* Prior Walter? The Bayeux tapestry Prior Walter?

PRIOR 1: His great-great-grandson. The fifth of the name.

PRIOR: I'm the thirty-fourth, I think.

PRIOR 1: Actually the thirty-second.

PRIOR: Not according to Mother.

PRIOR 1 *(Angry!)*: She's including the two bastards, then; I say leave them out. I say no room for bastards! The little things you swallow . . .

(The ghost snatches up a plastic pill bottle from Prior's night-stand.)

PRIOR: Pills.

PRIOR 1: Pills. For the pestilence. *(He struggles to open the bottle but can't get past the safety cap)* I too— *(He throws the bottle aside)*

PRIOR: Pestilence . . . You too what?

PRIOR 1: The pestilence in my time was much worse than now. Whole villages of empty houses. You could look outdoors and see Death walking in the morning, dew dampening the ragged hem of his black robe. Plain as I see you now.

PRIOR: You died of the plague.

PRIOR 1: The spotty monster. Like you, alone.

PRIOR: I'm not alone.

PRIOR 1: You have no wife, no children.

PRIOR: I'm gay.

PRIOR 1: So? Be gay, dance in your altogether for all I care, what's that to do with not having children?

PRIOR: Gay homosexual, not bonny, blithe and—never mind.

PRIOR 1: I had twelve. When I died.

(A second ghost appears, this one dressed in the clothing of an elegant seventeenth-century Londoner.)

PRIOR 1 *(Pointing to the new ghost)*: And I was three years younger than him.

(Prior sees the new ghost and screams!)

PRIOR: Oh God another one.

PRIOR 2: Prior Walter. Prior to you by some seventeen others.

PRIOR 1: He's counting the bastards.

PRIOR: Are we having a convention?

PRIOR 2: We've been sent to declare Her fabulous incipience. They love a well-paved entrance with lots of heralds, and—

PRIOR 1: The messenger come. Prepare the way. The infinite descent, a breath in air—

PRIOR 2: They chose us, I suspect, because of the mortal affinities. In a family as long-descended as the Walters there are bound to be a few carried off by plague.

PRIOR 1: The spotty monster.

PRIOR 2: Black Jack. Came from a water pump, half the city of London, can you imagine? His came from fleas. Yours, I understand, is the lamentable consequence of venery—

PRIOR 1: Fleas on rats, but who knew that?

PRIOR: Am I going to die?

PRIOR 2: We aren't allowed to discuss—

PRIOR 1: When you do, you don't get ancestors to help you through it. You may be surrounded by children but you die alone.

PRIOR: I'm afraid.

PRIOR 1 *(Grim)*: You should be. There aren't even torches, and the path's rocky, dark and steep.

PRIOR 2: Don't alarm him. There's good news before there's bad.

> We two come to strew rose petal and palm leaf before the triumphal procession. Prophet. Seer. Revelator. It's a great honor for the family.

PRIOR 1: He hasn't got a family.

PRIOR 2: I meant for the Walters, for the family in the larger sense.

PRIOR *(Singing)*:

> All I want is a room somewhere,
> Far away from the cold night air—

PRIOR 2 *(Putting a hand on Prior's forehead)*: Calm, calm, this is no brain fever . . .

> *(Prior keeps his eyes closed. The lights begin to change. Distant Glorious Music.)*

PRIOR 1 *(Low chant)*: Adonai, Adonai,
> Olam ha-yichud,
> Zefirot, Zazahot,
> Ha-adam, ha-gadol
> Daughter of Light,
> Daughter of Splendors,
> Fluor! Phosphor!
> Lumen! Candle!

PRIOR 2 (*Simultaneously, louder than Prior 1*): Even now,
    From the mirror-bright halls of Heaven,
    Across the cold and lifeless infinity of space,
    The Messenger comes
    Trailing orbs of light,
    Fabulous, incipient,
    Oh Prophet,
    To you!
PRIOR 1 AND PRIOR 2: Prepare, prepare,
    The Infinite Descent,
    A breath, a feather,
    Glory to—

(*They vanish.*)

Scene 2

The next day. Split scene: Prior in an exam room in an outpatient clinic at the hospital; he's seated on a stool, hooked up to a pentamidine IV drip. Louis and Belize facing one another at a table in a coffee shop. Louis, responding to something Belize has said, is pursuing an idea as he always does, by thinking aloud.

LOUIS: Why has democracy succeeded in America? Of course by succeeded I mean comparatively, not literally, not in the present, but what makes for the prospect of some sort of radical democracy spreading outward and growing up? Why does the power that was once so carefully preserved at the top of the pyramid by the original framers of the Constitution seem drawn inexorably downward and outward in spite of the best effort of the Right to stop this? I mean it's the really hard thing about being Left in this country, the American Left can't help but trip over all these petrified little fetishes: freedom, that's the worst; you know, *Jeane Kirkpatrick* for God's sake will go on and on about freedom and so what does that mean, the word "freedom," when she talks about it, or human rights; you have Bush talking about human rights, and so what are these people talking about, they might as well be talking about the mating habits of Venusians, these people don't begin to know what, ontologically, freedom is or human rights, like they see these bourgeois property-based Rights-of-Man-type rights but that's not enfranchisement, not democracy, not what's implicit, what's potential within the idea, not the idea with blood in it. That's just liberalism, the worst kind of liberalism, really, bourgeois tolerance, and what I think is that what AIDS shows us is the limits of tolerance, that it's not enough to be tolerated, because when the shit hits the fan you find out how much tolerance is worth. Nothing. And underneath all the tolerance is intense, passionate hatred.

BELIZE: Uh-huh.

LOUIS: Well don't you think that's true?

BELIZE: Uh-huh. It is.

LOUIS: *Power* is the object, not being tolerated. Fuck assimilation. But I mean in spite of all this the thing about America, I think, is that ultimately we're different from every other nation on earth, in that, with people here of every race, we can't— Ultimately what defines us isn't race, but politics. Not like any European country where there's an insurmountable fact of a kind of racial, or ethnic, monopoly, or monolith, like all Dutchmen, I mean Dutch people, are well, Dutch, and the Jews of Europe were never Europeans, just a small problem. Facing the monolith. But here there are so many small problems, it's really just a collection of small problems, the monolith is missing. Oh, I mean, of course I suppose there's the monolith of White America. White Straight Male America.

BELIZE: Which is not unimpressive, even among monoliths.

LOUIS: Well, no, but when the race thing gets taken care of— and I don't mean to minimalize how major it is, I mean I know it is, this is a really, really incredibly racist country but it's like, well, the British. I mean, all these blue-eyed pink people. And it's just weird, you know, I mean I'm not all that Jewish-looking, or . . . well, maybe I am but, you know, in New York, everyone is . . . well, not everyone, but so many are but so but in England, in London I walk into bars and I feel like Sid the Yid, you know I mean like Woody Allen in *Annie Hall*, with the payess and the gabardine coat, like never, never anywhere so much—I mean, not actively despised, not like they're Germans, who I think are still terribly anti-Semitic, and racist too, I mean black-racist, they pretend otherwise but, anyway, in London, there's just— And at one point I met this black gay guy from Jamaica who talked with a lilt but he said his family'd been living in London since before the Civil War—the American one—and how the English never let him forget for a minute that he wasn't blue-eyed and pink and I said yeah, me too, these people are anti-Semites and he said yeah but the British Jews have the clothing business all sewed up and blacks there can't get a foothold. And it was an incredibly awkward moment of just . . . I mean here we were, in this bar that was gay but it was a *pub*, you know, the beams and the plaster and those horrible little, like, two-day-old fish-

and-egg sandwiches—and just so British, so *old*, and
I felt, well, there's no way out of this because both of us
are, right now, too much immersed in this history, hope
is dissolved in the sheer age of this place, where race is
what counts and there's no real hope of change. It's the
racial destiny of the Brits that matters to them, not their
political destiny, whereas in America—

BELIZE: Here in America race doesn't count.

LOUIS: No, no, that's not—I mean you *can't* be hearing that.

BELIZE: I—

LOUIS: It's— Look, race, yes, but ultimately race here is a
political question, right? Racists just try to use race
here as a tool in a political struggle. It's not really about
race. Like the spiritualists try to use that stuff, are you
enlightened, are you centered, channeled, whatever, this
reaching out for a spiritual past in a country where no
indigenous spirits exist—only the Indians, I mean Native
American spirits and we killed them off so now, there are
no gods here, no ghosts and spirits in America, there are
no angels in America, no spiritual past, no racial past,
there's only the political, and the decoys and the ploys to
maneuver around the inescapable battle of politics, the
shifting downwards and outwards of political power to
the people—

BELIZE: POWER to the People! AMEN! *(Looking at his
watch) OH MY GOODNESS!* Will you look at the time,
I gotta—

LOUIS: Do you— You think this is, what, racist or naive or
something?

BELIZE: Well it's certainly *something*. Look, I just remembered
I have an appointment—

LOUIS: What? I mean I really don't want to, like, speak from
some position of privilege and—

BELIZE: I'm sitting here, thinking, eventually he's *got* to run out of steam, so I let you rattle on and on saying about maybe seven or eight things I find really offensive—

LOUIS: What?

BELIZE: But I know you, Louis, and I know the guilt fueling this peculiar tirade is obviously already swollen bigger than your hemorrhoids—

LOUIS: I don't have hemorrhoids.

BELIZE: I hear different. May I finish?

LOUIS: Yes, but I don't have hemorrhoids.

BELIZE: So finally, when I—

LOUIS: Prior told you— He's an asshole, he shouldn't have—

BELIZE: You promised, Louis. Prior is not a subject.

LOUIS: You brought him up.

BELIZE: I brought up hemorrhoids.

LOUIS: So it's indirect. Passive-aggressive.

BELIZE: Unlike, I suppose, banging me over the head with your theory that America doesn't have a race problem.

LOUIS: Oh be fair I never said that.

BELIZE: Not exactly, but—

LOUIS: I said—

BELIZE: —but it was close enough, because if it'd been that blunt I'd've just walked out and—

LOUIS: You deliberately misinterpreted! I—

BELIZE: Stop interrupting! I haven't been able to—

LOUIS: Just let me—

BELIZE: NO! What, talk? You've been running your mouth nonstop since I got here, yaddadda yaddadda blah blah blah, up the hill, down the hill, playing with your MONOLITH— *(Continue below:)*

LOUIS: Well, you could have joined in at any time instead of—

BELIZE *(Continuous from above)*: —and, girlfriend, it is truly an *awesome* spectacle but I got better things to do with my time than sit here listening to this racist bullshit just because I feel sorry for you that—

LOUIS: I am not a racist!

BELIZE: Oh come on!

LOUIS: So maybe I am a racist but—

BELIZE: Oh I really hate that! It's no fun picking on you Louis; you're so guilty, it's like throwing darts at a glob of jello, there's no satisfying hits, just quivering, the darts just blop in and vanish.

LOUIS: I just think when you are discussing lines of oppression it gets very complicated and—

BELIZE: Oh is that a fact? You know, we black drag queens have a rather intimate knowledge of the complexity of the lines of—

LOUIS: *Ex*-black drag queen.

BELIZE: Actually ex-ex.

LOUIS: You're doing drag again?

BELIZE: I don't— Maybe. I don't have to tell you. *Maybe.*

LOUIS: I think it's sexist.

BELIZE: I didn't ask you.

LOUIS: Well it is. The gay community, I think, has to adopt the same attitude towards drag as black women have to take towards black women blues singers.

BELIZE: Oh my we *are* walking dangerous tonight . . .

LOUIS: Well, it's all internalized oppression, right, I mean the masochism, the stereotypes, the—

BELIZE: Louis, are you deliberately trying to make me hate you?

LOUIS: No, I—

BELIZE: I mean, are you deliberately transforming yourself into an arrogant, sexual-political Stalinist-slash-racist flag-waving thug for my benefit?

(Pause.)

LOUIS: You know what I think?

BELIZE: What?

LOUIS: You hate me because I'm a Jew.

BELIZE: I'm leaving.

LOUIS: It's true.

BELIZE: You have no basis except your—

Louis, it's good to know you haven't changed; you are still an honorary citizen of the *Twilight Zone,* and after your pale, pale white polemics on behalf of racial insensitivity you have a flaming *fuck* of a lot of nerve calling me an anti-Semite. Now I really gotta go.

LOUIS: You called me Lou the Jew.

BELIZE: That was a joke.

LOUIS: I didn't think it was funny. It was hostile.

BELIZE: It was three years ago.

LOUIS: So?

BELIZE: You just called yourself Sid the Yid.

LOUIS: That's not the same thing.

BELIZE: Sid the Yid is different from Lou the Jew.

LOUIS: Yes.

BELIZE: Some day you'll have to explain that to me, but right now—

You hate me because you hate black people.

LOUIS: I do not. But I do think most black people are anti-Semitic.

BELIZE: "Most black people." *That's* racist, Louis, and *I* think most Jews—

LOUIS: Louis Farrakhan.

BELIZE: Ed Koch.

LOUIS: Jesse Jackson.

BELIZE: Jackson. Oh really, Louis, this is—

LOUIS: Hymietown! Hymietown!

BELIZE: Louis, you voted for Jesse Jackson! You send checks to the Rainbow Coalition!

LOUIS: I'm ambivalent. The checks bounced.

BELIZE: All your checks bounce, Louis; you're ambivalent about everything.

LOUIS: What's that supposed to mean?

BELIZE: You may be dumber than shit but I refuse to believe you can't figure it out. Try.

LOUIS: I was never ambivalent about Prior. I love him. I do. I really do.

BELIZE: Nobody said different.

LOUIS: Love and ambivalence are . . . Real love isn't ambivalent.

BELIZE: "Real love isn't ambivalent." I'd swear that's a line from my favorite bestselling paperback novel, *In Love with the Night Mysterious*, except I don't think you ever read it.

(Little pause.)

LOUIS: I never read it, no.

BELIZE: You ought to. Instead of spending the rest of your life trying to get through *Democracy in America*. It's about this white woman whose daddy owns a plantation in the Deep South in the years before the Civil War—the American one—and her name is Margaret, and she's in love with her daddy's number-one slave, and his name is Thaddeus, and she's married but her white slave-owner husband has AIDS: Antebellum Insufficiently Developed Sexorgans. And there's a lot of hot stuff going down when Margaret and Thaddeus can catch a spare torrid ten under the cotton-picking moon, and then of course the Yankees come, and they set the slaves free, and the slaves string up old daddy, and so on. Historical fiction. Somewhere in there I recall Margaret and Thaddeus find the time to discuss the nature of love. Her face is reflecting the flames of the burning plantation—you know, the way white people do—and his black face is dark in the night; and she says to him, "Thaddeus, real love isn't ever ambivalent."

(In the outpatient clinic, Emily enters, wearing latex gloves. She turns off Prior's IV drip.)

BELIZE: Thaddeus looks at her; he's contemplating her thesis; and he isn't sure he agrees.

(Emily removes the drip needle from Prior's arm and bandages the puncture wound.)

EMILY: Treatment number . . . *(Consulting chart)* four.
PRIOR: Pharmaceutical miracle. Lazarus breathes again.
LOUIS: Is he . . . How bad is he?
BELIZE: You want the laundry list?
EMILY: Shirt off, let's check the . . .

(Prior takes off his shirt. Emily examines his lesions.)

BELIZE: There's the weight problem and the shit problem and the morale problem.
EMILY: Only six. That's good. Pants.

(Prior removes his pants and underwear. He's naked. She examines his crotch, then he turns around and she examines his butt, looking for new lesions.)

BELIZE: And. He thinks he's going crazy.

(Prior puts his underwear back on.)

EMILY: Looking good. What else?

PRIOR: Ankles sore and swollen, but the leg's better. The nausea's mostly gone with the little orange pills. BM's pure liquid but not bloody anymore, for now, my eye doctor says everything's OK, for now, my dentist says, "Yuck!" when he sees my fuzzy tongue, and now he wears little condoms on his thumb and forefinger. And a mask. So what? My dermatologist is in Hawaii and my mother . . . well leave my mother out of it. Which is usually where my mother is, out of it. My glands are like walnuts, my weight's holding steady for week two, and a friend died two days ago of bird tuberculosis; bird tuberculosis; that scared me and I didn't go to the funeral today because he was an Irish Catholic and it's probably open casket and I'm afraid of . . . something, the bird TB or seeing him or . . . So I guess I'm doing OK. Except for of course I'm going nuts.

EMILY: We ran the toxoplasmosis series and there's no indication—

PRIOR: I know, I know, but I feel like something terrifying is on its way, you know, like a missile from outer space, and it's plummeting down towards the earth, and I'm ground zero, and . . . I am generally known where I am known as one cool, collected queen. And I am ruffled.

EMILY: There's really nothing to worry about. I think that shochen bamromim hamtzeh menucho nechono al kanfey haschino.

PRIOR: What?

EMILY: Everything's fine. Bemaalos k'doshim ut'horim kezohar horokeea mazhirim.

PRIOR: Oh I don't understand what you're—

EMILY: Es nishmas Prior sheholoch leolomoh, baavur shenod-
voo z'dokoh b'ad hazkoras nishmosoh—

PRIOR: WHY ARE YOU DOING THAT! Stop it! Stop it!

EMILY *(Shocked)*: Stop what?

PRIOR: You were just— Weren't you just speaking in Hebrew
or something.

EMILY: *Hebrew? (Laughs)* I'm basically Italian-American. No.
I didn't speak in Hebrew.

PRIOR: Oh no, oh God please I really think I—

EMILY: Look, I'm sorry, I have a waiting room full of—

(Prior starts dressing, frantic, terrified.)

EMILY: I think you're one of the lucky ones, you'll live for
years, probably—you're pretty healthy for someone with
no immune system. Are you seeing someone? Loneliness
is a danger. A therapist?

PRIOR: No, I don't need to see anyone, I just—

EMILY: Well think about it. You aren't going crazy. You're
just under a lot of stress. No wonder. *(She starts to write
in his chart)*

*(Suddenly there is an astonishing blaze of light and a menac-
ing subterranean rumble; then, a huge chord is sounded by a
gigantic choir, and a great book with steel pages mounted atop
a molten-red pillar bursts through the floor! In rapid succes-
sion: The book flies open! Instantly a large Aleph, inscribed
on the right-hand page, glows red and bursts into flames,
whereupon the book immediately slams shut, and with the
molten-red pillar it disappears in an eye blink under the floor,
as the lights restore to reveal the floor perfectly unmarred, not
a trace of its having been torn asunder. All of this occurs in*

95

under thirty seconds! Emily, making notes in Prior's file, has noticed none of this. Prior is agog.)

EMILY *(Laughing, exiting)*: Hebrew . . .

(Prior is paralyzed with fear. Then, partly undressed, he flees.)

LOUIS: Help me.

BELIZE: I beg your pardon?

LOUIS: You're a nurse, give me something, I . . . don't know what to do anymore, I . . . Last week at work I screwed up the Xerox machine like permanently and so I . . . Then I tripped on the subway steps and my glasses broke and I cut my forehead, here, see? And now I can't see much and my forehead—it's like the Mark of Cain, stupid, right, but it won't heal and every morning I see it and I think, Mark of Cain, Biblical things, people who . . . in betraying what they love betray what's truest in themselves, I feel . . . nothing but cold for myself, just cold. And every night I miss him, I miss him so much but then . . . those sores, and the smell and . . . where I thought it was going. I could be . . . I could be sick, too, maybe I'm sick, too. I don't know.

Belize. Tell him I love him. Can you do that?

BELIZE *(Tough, cold)*: I've thought about it for a very long time, and I still don't understand what love is. Justice is simple. Democracy is simple. Those things are unambivalent. But love is very hard. And it goes bad for you if you violate the hard law of love.

LOUIS: I'm dying.

BELIZE: *He's* dying. You just wish you were.

Oh cheer up, Louis. Look at that heavy sky out there.

LOUIS: Purple.

BELIZE: *Purple?* Boy, what kind of a homosexual are you, anyway? That's not purple, Mary, that color up there is *(Very grand)* mauve.

All day today it's felt like Thanksgiving. Soon, this . . . ruination will be blanketed white. You can smell it—can you smell it?

LOUIS: Smell what?

BELIZE: Softness, compliance, forgiveness, grace.

LOUIS: No . . .

BELIZE: I can't help you learn that. I can't help you, Louis. You're not my business. *(He exits)*

(Louis puts his head in his hands, inadvertently touching his cut forehead.)

LOUIS: Ow FUCK! *(He stands slowly, looks toward where Belize exited)* Smell what?
(He looks both ways to be sure no one is watching, then inhales deeply, and is surprised) Huh. Snow.

Scene 3

Harper in a very white, cold place, with a brilliant blue sky above; a delicate snowfall. She is dressed in a beautiful snowsuit. The sound of the sea, faint.

HARPER: Snow! Ice! Mountains of ice! Where am I? I . . . I feel better, I do, I . . . feel better. There are ice crystals in my lungs, wonderful and sharp. And the snow smells like cold, crushed peaches. And there's something . . .

97

some current of blood in the wind, how strange, it has that iron taste.

(Mr. Lies appears, also in splendid snowgear; his is emblazoned on the back with the IOTA logo.)

MR. LIES: Ozone.

HARPER: Ozone! Wow! Where am I?

MR. LIES: The Kingdom of Ice, the bottommost part of the world.

HARPER *(Looking around, then realizing)*: Antarctica. This is Antarctica!

MR. LIES: Cold shelter for the shattered. No sorrow here, tears freeze.

HARPER: Antarctica, Antarctica, oh boy oh boy, LOOK at this, I— Wow, I must've really snapped the tether, huh?

MR. LIES: Apparently . . .

HARPER: That's great. I want to stay here forever. Set up camp. Build things. Build a city, an enormous city made up of frontier forts, dark wood and green roofs and high gates made of pointed logs and bonfires burning on every street corner. I should build by a river. Where are the forests?

MR. LIES: No timber here. Too cold. Ice, no trees.

HARPER: Oh details! I'm sick of details! I'll plant them and grow them. I'll live off caribou fat, I'll melt it over the bonfires and drink it from long, curved goat-horn cups. It'll be great. I want to make a new world here. So that I never have to go home again.

MR. LIES: As long as it lasts. Ice has a way of melting.

HARPER: No. Forever. I can have anything I want here— maybe even companionship, someone who has . . . desire for me.

You, maybe.

MR. LIES: It's against the by-laws of the International Order of Travel Agents to get involved with clients. Rules are rules. Anyway, I'm not the one you really want.

HARPER: There isn't anyone . . . Maybe an Eskimo. Who could ice-fish for food. And help me build a nest for when the baby comes.

MR. LIES: There are no Eskimo in Antarctica. And you're not really pregnant. You made that up.

HARPER: Well all of this is made up. So if the snow feels cold I'm pregnant. Right? Here, I can be pregnant. And I can have any kind of a baby I want.

MR. LIES: This is a retreat, a vacuum, its virtue is that it lacks everything; deep-freeze for feelings. You can be numb and safe here, that's what you came for. Respect the delicate ecology of your delusions.

HARPER: You mean like no Eskimo in Antarctica.

MR. LIES: Correcto. Ice and snow, no Eskimo. Even hallucinations have laws.

HARPER: Well then who's that?

(The Eskimo appears.)

MR. LIES: An Eskimo.

HARPER: An Antarctic Eskimo. A fisher of the polar deep.

MR. LIES: There's something wrong with this picture.

(The Eskimo beckons.)

HARPER: I'm going to like this place. It's my own *National Geographic* Special! Oh! Oh! *(She holds her stomach)* I think . . . I think I felt her kicking. Maybe I'll give birth to a baby covered with thick white fur, and that way she won't be cold. My breasts will be full of hot cocoa so she

99

doesn't get chilly. And if it gets really cold, she'll have a pouch I can crawl into. Like a marsupial. We'll mend together. That's what we'll do; we'll mend.

Scene 4

Same day as Scene 2. Snowfall. An abandoned lot in the South Bronx. Trash around. A Homeless Woman is standing near an oil drum in which a fire is burning; she's sipping soup from a cloudy plastic container.

Hannah enters, frightened, angry and cold, dragging two heavy suitcases.

HANNAH: Excuse me? I said excuse me? Can you tell me where I am? Is this Brooklyn? Do you know a Pineapple Street? Is there some sort of bus or train or . . . ?

(The Homeless Woman looks at Hannah but doesn't respond. Hannah continues, trying to get through to her.)

HANNAH: I'm lost, I just arrived from Salt Lake. City. Utah?

(The Homeless Woman sips some soup. Hannah tries again.)

HANNAH: I took the bus that I was told to take and I got off— Well it was the very last stop, so I had to get off, and I *asked* the driver was this Brooklyn, and he nodded yes but he was from one of those foreign countries where they think it's good manners to nod at everything even if you have no idea what it is you're nodding at, and in truth I think he spoke no English at all, which I think would make him ineligible for employment on public transportation. The public being English-speaking, mostly. Do you speak English?

(The Homeless Woman nods. Hannah, realizing that the woman is crazy, looks around; seeing no one else in the desolate vicinity, she forges ahead.)

HANNAH: I was supposed to be met at the airport by my son. He didn't show and I don't wait more than three and three-quarters hours for *anyone*. I should have been patient, I guess, I . . . Is this—

HOMELESS WOMAN: Bronx.

HANNAH: Is that—The *Bronx*? Well how in the name of Heaven did I get to the Bronx when the bus driver said—

(The Homeless Woman turns to the empty air beside her and begins to berate it.)

HOMELESS WOMAN: Slurp slurp slurp will you STOP that disgusting slurping! YOU DISGUSTING SLURPING FEEDING ANIMAL! Feeding yourself, just feeding yourself, what would it matter, to you or to ANYONE, if you just stopped. Feeding. And DIED?

(Pause.)

HANNAH: Can you just tell me where I—

HOMELESS WOMAN *(To Hannah)*: Why was the Kosciuszko Bridge named after a Polack?

HANNAH: I don't know what you're—

HOMELESS WOMAN: That was a joke.

HANNAH: Well what's the punchline?

HOMELESS WOMAN: I don't know.

HANNAH *(Looking around desperately)*: Oh for pete's sake, is there anyone else who—

(The Homeless Woman turns again to the person she's hallucinating:)

HOMELESS WOMAN: Stand further off you fat loathsome whore! You can't have any more of this soup, slurp slurp slurp you animal, and the—I know you'll just go pee it all away and where will you do that? Behind what bush? It's FUCKING COLD out here and I—

Oh that's right, because it was supposed to have been a tunnel!

That's not very funny.

Have you read the prophecies of Nostradamus?

HANNAH: Who?

HOMELESS WOMAN: Some guy I went out with once somewhere, Nostradamus. Prophet, outcast, eyes like— Scary shit, he—

HANNAH: *Shut up.* Please! *(Taking a step closer to the Homeless Woman)* Now I want you to stop jabbering for a minute and pull your wits together and tell me how to get to Brooklyn. Because you know! And you are going to tell me! Because there is no one else around to tell me and I am wet and cold and I am very angry! So I am sorry you're psychotic but just make the effort. *(Another step closer)* Take a deep breath. DO IT!

(Hannah and the Homeless Woman breathe together.)

HANNAH: That's good. Now exhale.

(They do.)

HANNAH: Good. Now how do I get to Brooklyn?

HOMELESS WOMAN: Don't know. Never been. Sorry. Want some soup?

HANNAH: Manhattan? Maybe you know . . . *(Giving up: hopelessly)* I don't suppose you know the location of the Mormon Visitors'—

HOMELESS WOMAN: 65th and Broadway.

HANNAH: How do you—

HOMELESS WOMAN: Go there all the time. Free movies. Boring, but you can stay all day.

HANNAH: Well . . . So how do I—

HOMELESS WOMAN: Take the D train. Next block make a right.

HANNAH: Thank you.

(Hannah hoists her suitcases and starts to leave.)

HOMELESS WOMAN: Oh yeah.
    In the new century I think we will all be insane.

Scene 5

Same day. Joe and Roy in the living room of Roy's brownstone. Joe has just come in and is still in his coat. Roy wears an elegant bathrobe.

JOE: I can't. The answer's no. I'm sorry.

ROY: Oh, well, apologies.
    I can't see that there's anyone asking for apologies.

(Pause.)

JOE: I'm sorry, Roy.

ROY: Oh, well, apologies.

JOE: My wife is missing, Roy. My mother's coming from Salt Lake to . . . to help look, I guess. I'm supposed to be at the airport now, picking her up but . . . I just spent two days in a hospital, Roy, with a bleeding ulcer, I was spitting up blood.

ROY: Blood, huh? Look, I'm very busy here and—

JOE: It's just a job.

ROY: A job? A *job*? *Washington!* Dumb Utah Mormon hick shit!

JOE: Roy—

ROY: *WASHINGTON!* When Washington called me I was younger than you, you think I said, "Aw fuck no I can't go I got two fingers up my asshole and a little moral nosebleed to boot!" When Washington calls you my pretty young punk friend you go or you can go fuck yourself sideways 'cause the train has pulled out of the station, and you are *out*, nowhere, out in the cold. Fuck you, Mary Jane, get outta here.

JOE: Just let me—

ROY: Explain? Ephemera. You broke my heart. Explain that. Explain that.

JOE: I love you. Roy.

There's so much that I want, to be . . . what you see in me, I want to be a participant in the world, in your world, Roy, I want to be capable of that, I've tried, really I have but . . . I can't do this. Not because I don't believe in you, but because I believe in you so much, in what you stand for, at heart, the order, the decency. I would give anything to protect you, but . . . There are laws I can't break. It's too ingrained. It's not me. There's enough damage I've already done.

Maybe you were right, maybe I'm dead.

ROY: You're not dead, boy, you're a sissy.

You love me; that's moving, I'm moved. It's nice to be loved. I warned you about her, didn't I, Joe? But you don't listen to me, why, because you say Roy is smart and Roy's a friend but Roy . . . well, he isn't nice, and you wanna be nice. Right? A nice, nice man!

(Little pause)

You know what my greatest accomplishment was, Joe, in my life, what I am able to look back on and be proudest of? And I have helped make presidents and unmake them and mayors and more goddamn judges than anyone in NYC ever—AND several million dollars, tax-free—and what do you think means the most to me?

You ever hear of Ethel Rosenberg? Huh, Joe, huh?

JOE: Well, yeah, I guess I . . . Yes.

ROY: Yes. Yes. You have heard of Ethel Rosenberg. Yes. Maybe you even read about her in the history books.

If it wasn't for me, Joe, Ethel Rosenberg would be alive today, writing some personal-advice column for *Ms.* magazine. She isn't. Because during the trial, Joe, I was on the phone every day, talking with the judge—

JOE: Roy—

ROY: Every day, doing what I do best, talking on the telephone, making sure that timid Yid nebbish on the bench did his duty to America, to history. That sweet unprepossessing woman, two kids, boo-hoo-hoo, reminded us all of our little Jewish mamas—she came this close to getting life; I pleaded till I wept to put her in the chair. Me. I did that. I would have fucking pulled the switch if they'd have let me. Why? Because I fucking hate traitors. Because I fucking hate communists. Was it legal? Fuck legal. Am I a nice man? Fuck nice. They say terrible things about me in the *Nation*. Fuck the *Nation*. You want to be Nice, or you want to be Effective? Make the law, or subject to it. Choose. Your wife chose. A week from today, she'll be back. SHE knows how to get what SHE wants. Maybe I ought to send *her* to Washington.

JOE: I don't believe you.

ROY: Gospel.

JOE: You can't possibly mean what you're saying. Roy, you were the Assistant United States Attorney on the Rosenberg case, ex-parte communication with the judge during the trial would be . . . censurable, at least, probably conspiracy and . . . in a case that resulted in execution, it's . . .

ROY: What? *(Challenging)* Murder?

(Pause.)

JOE: You're not well is all.

ROY: What do you mean, not well? Who's not well?

(Pause.)

JOE: You said—

ROY: No I didn't. I said what?

JOE: Roy, you have cancer.

ROY: No I don't.

(Pause.)

JOE: You told me you were dying.

ROY: What the fuck are you talking about, Joe? I never said that. I'm in perfect health. There's not a goddamn thing wrong with me.
(He smiles)
Shake?

(Joe hesitates. He holds out his hand to Roy. Roy pulls Joe into a close, strong clench.)

ROY: It's OK that you hurt me because I love you, baby Joe. That's why I'm so rough on you.

(Roy releases Joe. Joe backs away a step or two.)

ROY: Prodigal son. The world will wipe its dirty hands all over you.
JOE: It already has, Roy.
ROY: Now go.

(Roy shoves Joe, hard. Joe turns to leave. Roy stops him, turns him around. He smooths the lapels on Joe's coat, tenderly.)

ROY: I'll always be here, waiting for you . . .

(Then with sudden violence, Roy grabs Joe's lapels and pulls him close, shaking him violently.)

ROY: What did you want from me?! What was all this?! What do you want, treacherous ungrateful little—

(Joe grabs Roy by the front of his robe, and propels him across the length of the room, slamming him against a bookcase. Joe holds Roy at arm's length, the other arm ready to hit.)

ROY *(Laughing softly, daring Joe)*: Transgress a little, Joseph.

(Joe releases Roy.)

ROY: There are so many laws; find one you can break.

(Joe hesitates, then turns and hurries out.
Roy doubles over in great pain, which he's been hiding
while Joe was in the room. As he sinks to the floor:)

ROY: Ah, Christ . . .
Andy! Andy! Get in here! Andy!

(The door opens, but it isn't Andy. A small Jewish woman
dressed modestly in a fifties hat and coat enters the room. The
room darkens.)

ROY: Who the fuck are you? The new nurse?

(The figure in the doorway says nothing. She stares at Roy.
A pause. Roy forces himself to stand, then he crosses to her.
He stares at her closely. Then he crosses back to a chair, and
sits heavily.)

ROY: Aw, fuck. Ethel.
ETHEL ROSENBERG *(Her manner is pleasant; her voice is ice-cold)*:
You don't look good, Roy.
ROY: Well, Ethel. I don't feel good.
ETHEL ROSENBERG: But you lost a lot of weight. That suits you.
You were heavy back then. Zaftig, mit hips.
ROY: I haven't been that heavy since 1960. We were all heavier
back then, before the body thing started. Now I look like
a skeleton. They stare.
ETHEL ROSENBERG: The shit's really hit the fan, huh, Roy?

(Roy nods.)

ETHEL ROSENBERG: Well the fun's just started.
ROY: What is this, Ethel, Halloween? You trying to scare me?

(Ethel says nothing.)

ROY: Well you're wasting your time! I'm scarier than you any day of the week! So beat it, Ethel! BOOO! BETTER DEAD THAN RED! Somebody trying to shake me up? HAH HAH! From the throne of God in Heaven to the belly of Hell, you can all fuck yourselves and then go jump in the lake because I'M NOT AFRAID OF YOU OR DEATH OR HELL OR ANYTHING!

ETHEL ROSENBERG: Be seeing you soon, Roy. Julius sends his regards.

ROY: Yeah, well send this to Julius!

(He flips the bird in her direction, stands and moves toward her, intending to slam the door in her face. Halfway across the room he collapses, in terrible abdominal pain.)

ETHEL ROSENBERG: You're a very sick man, Roy.

ROY: Oh God . . . ANDY!

ETHEL ROSENBERG: Hmmm. He doesn't hear you, I guess. We should call the ambulance.
(She goes to the phone)
Hah! Buttons! Such things they got now.
What do I dial, Roy?

(Pause. Roy looks at her, then:)

ROY: 911.

ETHEL ROSENBERG *(Dials the phone)*: It sings!
(Imitating dial tones) La la la . . .
Huh.
Yes, you should please send an ambulance to the home of Mr. Roy Cohn, the famous lawyer.
Beats me. A pain in his gut. Bad. A bad pain.
What's the address, Roy?

ROY *(A beat, then)*: 244 East 87th.

ETHEL ROSENBERG: 244 East 87th Street. No apartment number, he's got the whole building.

  My name? *(A beat)* Ethel Greenglass Rosenberg.

  (Small smile) Me? No I'm not related to Mr. Cohn.
An old friend.

  (She hangs up)

  They said a minute.

ROY: I have all the time in the world.

ETHEL ROSENBERG: You're immortal.

ROY: I'm immortal. Ethel. *(He wills himself to his feet)*

  I have *forced* my way into history. I ain't never gonna die.

ETHEL ROSENBERG: History is about to crack wide open.
Millennium approaches.

Scene 6

*That night, Prior's bedroom. Prior, in bed, even more frightened
than before. Prior 1 stands before him, wearing a weird hat and
robes ornamented with strange signs over his coarse farmer's tunic.
He carries a long palm-leaf bundle.*

PRIOR 1: Tonight's the night! Aren't you excited? Tonight She
arrives! Right through the roof! Ha-adam, ha-gadol . . .

PRIOR 2 *(Appearing, similarly attired)*: Lumen! Phosphor!
Fluor! Candle! An unending billowing of scarlet and—

(Prior flings off his covers. He's prepared.)

PRIOR: Look. Garlic. A mirror. Holy Water. *(He squirts water
at Prior 1 from a small plastic squirt bottle)* A crucifix.
FUCK OFF! Get the fuck out of my room! GO!

PRIOR 1 *(Leering a little; to Prior 2)*: Hard as a hickory knob, I'll bet.

PRIOR 2: We all tumesce when they approach. We wax full, like moons.

PRIOR 1 *(A barked command)*: Dance.

PRIOR: Dance?

PRIOR 1: Stand up, damnit, give us your hands, dance!

PRIOR 2: Listen . . .

(A lone oboe begins to play a little dance tune.)

PRIOR 2: Delightful sound. Care to dance?

PRIOR: Please leave me alone, please just let me sleep.

PRIOR 2: Ah, he wants someone familiar. A partner who knows his steps. *(To Prior)* Close your eyes. Imagine . . .

PRIOR: I don't—

PRIOR 2: Hush. Close your eyes.

(Prior does.)

PRIOR 2: Now open them.

(Prior does.
Louis appears. He looks gorgeous. The dance tune transitions into a lovely instrumental version of "Moon River.")

PRIOR: Lou.

LOUIS: Dance with me.

PRIOR: I can't, my leg, it hurts at night.
Are you . . . a ghost, Lou?

LOUIS: No. Just spectral. Lost to my self. Sitting all day on cold park benches. Wishing I could be with you. Dance with me, babe . . .

(Prior stands, gingerly putting weight on his bad leg. He's surprised there's no pain. He walks to Louis.
They begin to dance. The music is beautiful.)

PRIOR 1 *(To Prior 2)*: Hah. Now I see why he's got no children. He's a sodomite.

PRIOR 2: Oh be quiet, you medieval gnome, and let them dance.

PRIOR 1: I'm not interfering, I've done my bit. Hooray, hooray, the messenger's come, now I'm blowing off. I don't like it here.

(Prior 1 vanishes. Prior 2 watches Louis and Prior dance.)

PRIOR 2: The twentieth century. Oh dear, the world has gotten so terribly, terribly old.

(Prior 2 vanishes. Louis and Prior dance.
Louis vanishes.
Prior dances alone, his arms holding empty air, as if not realizing that Louis has gone.
The lights return to normal.
Then suddenly, the sound of the beating of enormous wings.
Prior opens his eyes. The pain in his leg returns.)

Scene 7

Same night, continuous with Scene 6. Split scene: Prior alone in his apartment; Louis alone in the park.
Again, the sound of beating wings.

PRIOR *(Looking up in terror at the ceiling)*: Oh don't come in here don't come in—

(Limping back to his bed. Scared, broken, he calls out)
Louis!

(Summoning defiance) No! My name is Prior Walter, I am . . . the scion of an ancient line, I am . . . abandoned I— NO. My name is . . . is . . . *Prior* and I live . . . *here and now*, and—

(The lights in the room intensify slightly as, to Prior's horror, an inhuman voice comes out of his mouth:)

PRIOR: —*in the dark, in the dark, the Recording Angel opens its hundred eyes and snaps the spine of the Book of Life and*—

(Prior clamps his hand over his mouth; the lights return to normal.)

PRIOR: Hush! Hush! I'm talking nonsense, I—

(Trying to calm himself) No more mad scene, hush, hush . . .

(Louis is on a bench in Central Park. Joe approaches, stands at a distance. They stare at each other. Louis stands.)

LOUIS: Do you know the story of Lazarus?

JOE: Lazarus?

LOUIS: Lazarus. I can't remember what happens, exactly.

JOE: I don't . . . Well, he was dead, Lazarus, and Jesus breathed life into him. He brought him back from death.

LOUIS: Come here often?

JOE: No. Yes. Yes.

LOUIS: Back from the dead. You believe that really happened?

JOE: I don't know anymore what I believe.

LOUIS: This is quite a coincidence. Us meeting.

JOE: I followed you.
    From work. I . . . followed you here.

(Little pause.)

LOUIS: You followed me.
    You probably saw me that day in the washroom and
    thought: there's a sweet guy, sensitive, cries for friends
    in trouble.
JOE: Yes.
LOUIS: You thought maybe I'll cry for you.
JOE: Yes.
LOUIS: Well I fooled you. Crocodile tears. *(He touches his heart,
    shrugs, then harshly)* Nothing.

(Joe reaches tentatively to touch Louis's face. Louis pulls back.)

LOUIS: What are you doing? Don't do that.

*(Joe withdraws his hand and takes several steps back, ready
to run.)*

JOE: Sorry. I'm sorry.
LOUIS: I'm . . . just not— *(Warning him away)* I think, if you
    touch me, your hand might fall off or something. Worse
    things have happened to people who have touched me.
JOE: Please.

(Joe walks up to Louis.)

JOE: Oh, boy . . .
    Can I . . .

I . . . want . . . to touch you. Can I please just touch you . . . um, here?

(He puts his hand on one side of Louis's face. He holds it there.)

JOE: I'm going to Hell for doing this.
LOUIS: Big deal. You think it could be any worse than New York City?

(Louis takes Joe's hand away from his face and holds it, then:)

LOUIS: Come on.
JOE: Where?
LOUIS: Home. With me.
JOE: This makes no sense. I mean I don't know you.
LOUIS: Likewise.
JOE: And what you do know about me you don't like.
LOUIS: The Republican stuff?
JOE: Yeah, well for starters.
LOUIS *(Meaning it)*: I don't not like that. I *hate* that.
JOE: So why on earth should we—

(Louis kisses Joe.)

LOUIS: Strange bedfellows. I don't know. I never made it with one of the damned before.
I would really rather not have to spend tonight alone.
JOE: I'm a pretty terrible person, Louis.
LOUIS: Lou.

(Joe steps back from Louis.)

JOE: No, I really really am. I don't think I deserve being loved.

LOUIS *(A nod)*: There? See? We already have a lot in common.

> *(Louis begins to walk away. He turns, looks back at Joe. Joe follows. They exit.*
>
> *Prior listens. At first he hears nothing, then all at once, the sound of beating wings again, now frighteningly near. Prior stares up at the ceiling, terrified.)*

PRIOR: That sound, that sound, it . . . *What is that*, like birds or something, like a really *big* bird, I'm frightened, I . . . No! No fear, find the anger, find the . . . anger! *(Standing on the bed, fierce, up at the ceiling)* My blood is clean, my brain is fine, I can handle pressure, I am a gay man and I am used to pressure, to trouble, I am tough and strong and . . . Oh. Oh my goodness. I . . . *(He is washed over by an intense sexual feeling)* Ooohhhh . . . I'm hot, I'm . . . so . . . *(He sinks to his knees)* Aw Jeez what is going on here I . . . must have a fever, I—

> *(The bedside lamp flickers wildly! Prior screams. Then the bed begins to lurch violently back and forth. The room is filled with a deep bass creaking and groaning, like the timbers of a ship under immense stress, coming from the ceiling. The bed stops moving as the creaking and groaning sounds intensify; the bedside lamp glows brighter and brighter as, from the ceiling, there's a fine rain of plaster dust.)*

PRIOR: OH! PLEASE, OH PLEASE! Something's coming in here, I'm scared, I don't like this at all, something's approaching and I—

> *(There is a great blaze of triumphal music, heralding.)*

PRIOR: OH!

(Four thunderous chords sound, and with each chord the bedroom is saturated with colored light: first, extraordinary, harsh, cold, pale blue; then, rich, brilliant, warm gold; then, hot, bilious green; and finally, spectacular royal purple. Then there's silence for several beats. Prior stares wildly around the purple-colored room.)

PRIOR *(An awestruck whisper)*: God almighty.
  Very Steven Spielberg.

(A sound, like a plummeting meteor, tears down from very, very far above the earth, hurtling at an incredible velocity toward the bedroom. The light seems to be sucked out of the room as the projectile approaches. Right before the light is completely extinguished, there's a terrifying CRASH as something immense strikes earth. The bedroom shudders and pieces of the ceiling's plaster, lathe and wiring rain down on and around Prior's bed; as the room is plunged into absolute darkness, we hear the whole ceiling give way.

  A beat, and then, in a shower of unearthly white light, spreading great opalescent gray-silver wings, the Angel descends through the ceiling into the room and floats above the bed.)

ANGEL: Greetings, Prophet;
  The Great Work begins:
  The Messenger has arrived.

(Blackout.)

END OF PART ONE

A Few Notes from the Playwright About Staging

In General

Millennium Approaches and *Perestroika* are two parts of a single play, but at the same time they're two rather different plays, each with its own structure and character. *Millennium* has three acts and *Perestroika* has five. Three acts make a tauter, cleaner play, the gestures and rhythms of which will feel more inexorable, more destination-driven; a five-act play is likely to provide a more expansive, exploratory and ultimately open-ended and unresolved experience. Perhaps it can be said that *Millennium* is a play about security and certainty being blown apart, while *Perestroika* is about danger and possibility following the explosion. The events in *Perestroika* proceed from the wreckage made by the Angel's traumatic entry at the end of *Millennium*. A membrane has broken; there is disarray and debris. All of which is to suggest that, especially when the two parts of *Angels* are produced in repertory, the differences should be visible and palpable onstage.

The plays benefit from a pared-down style of presentation, with scenery kept to an evocative and informative minimum. There are a lot of scenes and a lot of locations; an informative minimum means providing what's needed to enable the audience to know, as quickly as possible, where a scene is set. Actors need to help by playing the reality of these locations: How loud can you get, really, in a fancy restaurant?

I recommend rapid scene shifts (no blackouts!), employing the cast as well as stagehands in shifting the scene. This must be an actor-driven event.

Intermissions

Audiences are said to have grown increasingly impatient and unwilling to sit through long evenings in the theater. The people of whom this is true will likely seek out shorter plays than *Angels in America*. I believe that, once engaged, audiences rediscover the rewards of patience and effort and the pleasures of an epic journey. An epic play *should* be a little fatiguing; a rich, heady, hard-earned fatigue is among a long journey's pleasures and rewards.

That said, the audience has to be given chances along the way to gather its strength and attention. *Millennium Approaches* is a long play, and *Perestroika* is longer. Each play is meant to have two intermissions, after Act One and Act Two of *Millennium*, and after Act Three and Act Four of *Perestroika*. These segments are shaped to function as coherent single events as well as successions of scenes.

The temptation to take only one intermission in each of the two parts should, in my opinion, be resisted. Although one intermission shortens the running time, the demands it puts on the audience's attention and the pressures it puts on the scenes immediately before the single intermission or near the end of the play are unnecessary, detrimental and counter-productive—the running time may be shorter, but it will feel much longer.

Magic

The moments of magic, such as the appearance and disappearance of Mr. Lies, the ghosts, Prior's fiery Book hallucination and the Angel's arrival, ought to be fully imagined and realized, as wonderful *theatrical* illusions—which means it's OK if the wires show, and maybe it's good that they do, but the magic should at the same time be thoroughly thrilling, fantastical, amazing.

It's easy to stage a person's (or a ghost's) magical disappearance by simply having the actor exit into the wings, but I don't think that's a strong choice. Not only is it *not* thoroughly thrilling, fantastical, amazing or fun to watch a person walk offstage, it's also pedestrian, literally and figuratively. Walking offstage is slow, and therefore it lacks one very important aspect of *vanishing*—namely that it's abrupt. In a world in which young people by their thousands sicken and, with obscene speed, die (in other words, the world of this play), vanishing abruptly is particularly upsetting, even frightening. The magic ought to be fun for the audience, but also disturbing. For Prior, it's increasingly terrifying.

There's more magic in *Perestroika*, and as the play progresses, the magic gets grander. It's hard to make this happen: long, two-part plays are enormously demanding of resources, time and energy, and there's always the risk that invention, attention to detail, time and cash will run out just when they're needed most, in the play's home stretch. *Perestroika*'s fifth-act Heaven scenes should, whether or not the stage directions are followed, at the very least resemble nothing on Earth; the Hall of the Continental Principalities in Act Five, Scene 5, ought to be the high point of the stage magic of *Angels*.

Split Scenes

In the split scenes, two separate events occur more or less simultaneously in different locations—for example, Act One, Scene 8, of *Millennium Approaches*, in which we observe Harper and Joe in their living room in Brooklyn and Louis and Prior in their Alphabetland bedroom. Both events are intended to continue, active and alive, throughout the entire split scene, with focus going where the story needs it to go. Stopping one of the two events in its tracks by artificially freezing it is an easy but again, in my opinion, not a strong choice. The trick is to work out psychologically coherent (hence playable), compellingly dramatic reasons why the characters in one event become still and quiet when the action that the audience should be attending to shifts to the other event and onto other characters.

When a character chooses to stop talking, to be still and quiet, for reasons having to do with the conflict he or she is in during a scene, an active choice is being made, and hence the character stays alive onstage—as opposed to being put in suspended animation by the director. Finding concurrent, complementary vitality in the two events of a split scene gives them their particular dynamism; they'll be much more fun to play, and to watch.

Language

The engine of the play is the struggle in which the characters engage to change unendurable circumstances—*all* the characters, *all* the time we're watching them. The circumstances the characters face, the world they inhabit, and the characters themselves are in a very important sense made up of words.

Words are important, and they're specific. We speak to produce effects, to catalyze, to engender consequences. We choose words strategically, precisely, whether or not we do so consciously.

If the character you're playing says something that strikes you, the actor, as odd, large, artificial, you should assume it strikes your character that way as well. If a character opposite yours says something that sounds ornate, awkward, a non-sequitur to you, the actor, it probably sounds that way to your character too.

I advise taking very seriously and working hard to answer the question that you, the actor, and probably also the character you're playing, are longing to ask: Why am I/Why is this other person talking this way? That question is important. When the language in the play is strange, in other words, its strangeness is always an action. A sentence is no less an action than a blow with a broadsword or a passionate kiss. And the degree and kind of strangeness matter enormously.

The characters in the play are fighting for survival; the stakes are very high. They talk to make things happen, to advance an agenda, to defend, to enlist, to seduce, to punish. Sometimes they speak in an effort to understand how or what they're feeling. But never speak solely to announce your character's distress, hoping for pity. The characters in the play are tougher than that; the world of the play, like the world outside the theater, is a tough place.

Two Notes Regarding Pronunciation

On page 20, Roy's coinage, "azido-methatalo-molamoca-whatchamacallit" is pronounced "aZIDOmuhTHATUHLO-moluhmocuh-whatchamacallit." The "I" in "ZIDO" is short, as in "in," and the "TH" in "*THA*TUHLO" is soft, as in "*TH*istle."

On page 88, Prior is using the verb "prophesy," which is pronounced "proph-uh-sigh," *not* the noun "prophecy" which is pronounced "proph-uh-see."

Nine Notes Regarding the Angel

The Angel, who is related to humans but isn't human, is arguably the most challenging character in *Angels*, and Act Two of *Perestroika* is inarguably the most challenging sequence. After two decades of struggling with her and watching others struggle, I'm offering these thoughts, which I hope will be helpful.

1) *Metaphysics:* I'll begin by repeating: The Angel is related to humans but isn't human. That's the primary challenge in acting, directing and designing her. For starters, she refers to herself in the plural (I I I I) because she isn't a single thing: She is a Principality, which is, depending on which angelological ordering system you subscribe to, the highest or one of the highest types among the angelic orders. She is four Divine Emanations—Lumen (blue), Candle (gold), Phosphor (green) and Fluor (purple)—manifest as an aggregate entity, the Continental Principality of America. I have no advice about how to play four nonhuman beings amalgamated into one nonhuman being. I only know that while she should be comprehensible to the audience, she should also be terribly unfamiliar.

2) *Appearance:* She should be extraordinary to behold, and her wings are of paramount importance—they should move and they should move us. She shouldn't look like Botticelli painted her, or any other Italian Renaissance painter, or any European of any period, or like a traditional Christmas tree ornament. She should look breathtaking, severe, scary, powerful, and magnificently American.

3) *Her Cough:* The Angel's cough is a manifestation of cosmic unwellness, but she controls it, and she is a creature of unimaginable strength and discipline. She doesn't want Prior to sense any weakness, disorder or confusion on her part, and her cough ought to be a single, dry bark, *not* prolonged wracking emphysemic spasms. Ellen McLaughlin, who created the role, based her brusque, even angry rap of a cough on a cat hacking up a furball. It was startling, sharp, simple—one *hack*, not ten—and effectively nonhuman, not funny as much as disconcerting and ominous, and always always *dignified*. It did not make her seem frail.

4) *She's Not Joking, and She's No Joke:* Some of what happens between Prior and the Angel is supposed to be funny, but it's essential for the play, and, for that matter, for the comedy, that the Angel's dignity and her unequivocally serious purpose are never—as in *not for one single second!*—compromised by schticky winking at the audience. Prior's terror at being in her presence and/or at the possibility that he's going mad never (as in not for one single second) abandons him. As Prior has his first full encounter with the Angel, and simultaneously relates it to Belize three weeks later, we're watching a cosmically high-stakes encounter between a badly frightened but very brave human being and his furious, grief-stricken, frightened and frighteningly powerful nonhuman visitor/intruder.

Apologies if I'm sounding strident, but I've learned that there are dire consequences if this reality is parodied or traduced. People can enjoy pratfalls, mugging and easy laughs, even while determining that they won't be fooled again into deep investment in what's proved to be unserious. Once faith in the seriousness of what's onstage has been withdrawn, however briefly, it's unlikely to return fully.

5) *Her Arrival:* If at all technically feasible, the Angel should arrive in Prior's bedroom by crashing through the ceiling. This is harder than bringing her through a crack in the rear wall, which is what's usually done. But she's coming down from Heaven, not from across town; it's a drop-down-on-your-head explosive revelation, rather than the sneaky, sideways kind. If at all possible, she should arrive in dust and noise as the ceiling rains down on Prior's head. I didn't know, when I wrote the play, that so few theaters have fly space.

6) *Flying Versus Rehearsing*: I also didn't know how difficult stage flying would prove to be. Originally I imagined that the Angel would fly during Act Two of *Perestroika*, doing spectacular aerial stunts as she spoke. I've seen many productions of *Perestroika*, and I've never seen this happen. What I've seen instead is many valuable hours of rehearsal and tech time lost, and much money spent hiring stage-flying specialists, trying to make this happen.

I've come to the conviction that attempting extensive flying is not only unwise, because it lies beyond the technical and temporal means of most theaters, it's a distraction from the real business at hand. The Anti-Migratory Epistle sequence in Act Two won't be solved by Angelic midair somersaults—which, trust me, will never materialize. The effectiveness of this long and difficult scene depends entirely on getting its complex realities clear, specific and playable, and that means time-consuming, painstaking, actor-director rehearsal-room work, for which there is no substitute.

7) *Unhooking the Angel:* There *should* be flying, of course: The Angel should fly in, and fly out, carrying the Epistle. In between her entrance and her exit, she has to be able to move around the stage, so that she can interact fully with Prior and, when appropriate, with Belize. This most likely means that she will have to be unhooked from her flying rig onstage while the scene is in progress, and then hooked back up. Stagehands, visible to the audience, can do this. Her fly-wires show, so why not visible stagehands? Stagehands ought to help Prior out of his prophet garb and into his pajamas in the transition from the street to his bedroom and back again.

Openly including the crew in the stage life in Act Two (when necessary for the storytelling, not as an embellishment) seems to me consonant with the act's mixing narrated and dramatized storytelling, an amalgam which occurs at no other point in *Angels*. Moments when the crew takes active part in the dramatic event should be staged—interesting to watch, specific and unapologetic, not artificially slow but not rushed and frantic. Prior's change of clothes, from prophet drag to pajamas, is part of a transition he's chosen to undertake. He's stepping into a violent memory because telling Belize isn't enough; Prior has to show him. When the stagehands unhook the Angel, they should do so respectfully; it goes without saying that they wouldn't touch her without her willing them to do so.

8) *Staging the Anti-Migratory Epistle:* Act Two confronts directors, actors and designers with the formidable (but, I hope, exciting and enjoyable) challenge of staging three characters

occupying two locations that are separated, albeit permeably and not cleanly, by distance and time.

This is a scene involving *three* characters: Prior, the Angel and Belize. There's a temptation to sideline Belize to a stationary spot on the outskirts and leave him there for the duration, tossing in quips, irrelevant to the action. This is a tempting choice because it makes the scene easier to stage. The problem is that without Belize's active involvement, the scene makes no sense. The overarching actions are the Angel's arrival, the delivery of the Epistle, Prior's refusal of it, and then his unwilling acceptance of or forced submission to it. But the scene takes place in the present as well as in the past, and integral to the event is the in-the-bedroom/on-the-street contest between Belize and the Angel for Prior's attention and soul, a battle of three strong wills that propels/pulls Belize into Prior's bedroom, into his awful dream—where, once he's entered, the Angel seems intermittently to be aware of Belize's presence.

Belize is tough, but Prior unfolds for him what must sound, to a nurse with considerable experience dealing with AIDS, like a wholly unfamiliar form of dementia, far more coherent than anything Belize has heard from his patients. He's bewildered, grief-stricken, and, when Prior's delusions assume uncharacteristically, deeply disturbing reactionary, even racist overtones, Belize becomes frightened and then angry. Thus Prior's desperate attempt to end his loneliness by telling his best friend about the waking nightmare in which he's trapped results in even greater isolation.

9) *Her Broken Heart:* The Angel's power and purpose semi-successfully conceal an abandoned lover's determination to get her lost love to return before everything falls apart. Prior is supposed to be useful, as surrogate for his species, the last fragile hope of averting universal extinction. But to the heart-

broken lover that this heavenly emissary also is, he's a hateful, guilty homewrecker who also happens to be her kin and her ward. In this predicament the Angel is recognizable to Prior, to Belize and to us, and she grows more familiar as the Epistle progresses, but only to a point. As I began, so I'll end: the Angel isn't human.

CPSIA information can be obtained
at www.ICGtesting.com
Printed in the USA
LVHW020306060820
662515LV00006B/1789

9 780881 456516